Our Christian Faith

OUR CHRISTIAN FAITH

Answers for the Future

Karl Rahner & Karl-Heinz Weger

Crossroad · New York

copy 1

Preface

This preface has not been written simply because prefaces are customary. The authors of the book feel they owe the reader a few words of explanation about the aim and the limitations of the remarks presented here, since they represent an exchange of views between a "new generation" and theologians that is unusual in religious writing. Concentration on the fundamental religious questions of our time (that is, the questions the answers to which were in the past the automatic inheritance of the faithful) has produced an alternation of enquiries and answers which honestly formulates rarely expressed (but nonetheless burdensome) questions asked by Christians today, and offers equally honest answers. Such at least is the hope of the authors.

The outlook of the present, of the "new generation", is largely marked by resigned scepticism. However, the term "new generation" in this connection is hard to define exactly. Perhaps it is the younger generation which the psychologist Victor E. Frankl mainly has in mind when he says: Every period has its neurosis—and every period needs its psychotherapy. Today we are no longer confronted, as in Freud's day, with a sexual, but with an existential frustration. And the typical patient today is suffering not so much, as in Adler's day, from an inferiority complex, but from a meaninglessness complex, associated with a feeling of emptiness.

This is the emptiness of the replete, who have been overfed with beliefs, world-views and religious offers, to whom the

Christian faith appears as only one of the many opinions going cheap in the world religion market. But the search for a meaning to life in the midst of an achieving society whose limits are beginning to become obvious does not affect only the younger generation. It has no less an effect on the "middle generation", and for this reason the religious questions of the "new generation" do not really correlate with age. The loud laughter provoked by Nietzsche's "madman" who went around on a bright morning with a lighted lamp looking for God is today the lot of many people who sincerely profess any faith.

Why? First because it looks as though no one is quite so sure of his or her position? How could one be, when others claim the same sort of certainty for their faith or world-view? Secondly, one constantly finds it more difficult to avoid the question of value and usefulness, of the credibility of religious or philosophical beliefs. Are they any more than an ideological superstructure on top of life, which one has to live anyway and which one must allow to flow over one without getting any real help? This "superstructure" is what this book is about. We try, by means of questions and answers, to set out the basis and object of the Christian faith in such a way that the reader feels understood. The questions are not all on the same level. The answers do not solve all the problems. The authors do not entertain the illusion that at the end everything is fine and no individual with even a little good will should have any more questions. If the general nature and the essence of the Christian faith become a little clearer, and if answers are given to questions which are normally hardly ever asked and therefore hardly ever answered, this book will have served its purpose.

A few technical remarks. The book was not intended either as an exchange of letters or as an imitation of one, even though the arguments are presented in question and answer form.

As far as the "enquiries" are concerned, we had to limit ourselves to what seemed essential. Not everything which might—quite properly—be questioned today could be discussed. It may be that for this reason the reader will not find his or her problems dealt with, or not dealt with in sufficient detail.

Unfortunately subjective interests (in this case those of the authors) can never be totally excluded. Something else which readers may find more irritating is that the questioner presents his enquiries from different positions, at one point more as a "worried atheist", then as a "fringe Catholic", and finally as a person who makes no secret of being a professional theologian. We have deliberately avoided the creation of a single literary identity, in order to speak to the widest possible range of readers.

A more difficult problem is raised by the answers given to the enquiries. First, each of the enquiries contains a mass of material only some of which can be dealt with. Since we did not plan to write a long book, only the most important points could be picked out, and here again a reader may wish for a more detailed comment on one question or another. On the other hand, no important question has been evaded, and of necessity some topics must be left as a stimulus to individual reflection and further study. In ultimate religious questions above all, there are no ready final answers which a person can simply adopt without personal effort and assimilation. The authors also hope that readers will understand why the answers could not be taken up again and re-examined in the subsequent enquiries. Such an approach would have gone way beyond the bounds of this book's possibilities.

For the sake of directness, each chapter is written as if addressed to the reader by an individual. This mode of address does not negate the book's dual authorship.

The concluding section of the book, written by Karl Rahner, is a modified form of an article which appeared in 1972 in *Meyers Enzyklopädisches Lexikon,* vol. V (Mannheim 1972), pp. 672–7.

The authors continue to hope that this book will be an aid to faith. With that hope they wish to combine a particular word of thanks to Mrs. Elisabeth von der Lieth for her unsparing help.

Karl Rahner
Karl-Heinz Weger

One

Why believe at all?

M y problem—and let us make this the subject of the first discussion—is not so much the "what" and the content of the Christian faith. My problem is the "why" of faith. I know, of course, that one can't ask "why?" without taking the content into account, and there will be plenty of opportunity to examine the contents of faith as such. As far as the contents of faith are concerned, indeed, I can be both petty and generous. Petty, when I can't make sense of an article of faith and it simply has to be believed because it's there. But mostly generous: a few dogmas more or less don't make any difference to me. If there were ten sacraments instead of seven, it wouldn't affect my "faith nerve". But the "why" of faith! That makes me want to give up. Surely real faith ought to burn! Ought it not to drive us on to the streets? Ought it not to want to convince others, not out of arrogance or superiority, but out of the certainty of a meaning found and a happiness experienced? At least from a sense of satisfaction and inner peace? Not that I want to bring back the days of the wars of religion—though when people cracked skulls (literally and metaphorically) on account of matters of religion, there must have been something at the bottom of it. In those days people must have argued, quarrelled, become enemies and hated each other because they believed there was something at stake. And now? The Christian faith provides no inspiration, exerts no fascination, arouses no enthusiasm. Not in me and not in others. What other explanation is there for the reluctance of young people in particular to commit themselves to the Christian faith. In saying this I don't mean to conceal the fact that I see no real alternative to the Christian faith. I want to be a Christian, and I can find a fragment of commitment in me even when someone tries to treat me as a bit antiquated or primitive because of my Christian faith, when it is assumed that a "rational", "progressive", "scientific" person obviously couldn't be anything but an atheist. When I look at the arguments of the atheists—and I know them—they're a pretty thin brew.

So let no one tell me that "people" today can't rationally and honestly believe in God or be Christians. And yet this commitment is based on a defensive attitude. My pride, perhaps even my ordinary common sense, is insulted. But inside, where something ought to be burning, there's nothing burning. Where there ought to be shouting, there is emptiness and silence.

The Christian faith lives on the hope of the resurrection, the beatific vision of God. That is the goal of a human life. That is what we live, work and suffer for. And the joys of human existence are like the anticipations of eternal happiness. That is the Church's message. I don't want to discuss here how credible the disciples' Easter experiences are. Even before this we are brought up against an unpleasant fact, the fact of an inner resistance and revolt against survival after death. Christ has risen from the dead. All right, but what's it got to do with me? Will I rise from the dead—no thanks. If after death it was the end of everything, that would be fine by me. To be nothing after death is just the same as before birth. You can't say anything more about this non-existence. It is neither attractive nor horrible, neither a gain nor a loss. Nothing, simply nothing. To die, to sleep: Hamlet's wish! (And by the way, aren't an extraordinary number of people these days turning to Buddhism? And isn't it precisely the doctrine of Nirvana, the absorption of the individual life into nothingness, which makes this "religion" attractive?) But however that may be, Christianity certainly offers me an end, a fulfilment and a future for which I have absolutely no desire. I don't want this offer. Not even because I find the price too high. Any halfway decent life exacts some price or other. It's not the price, it's the idea. Why doesn't God just leave us alone? Why won't he let us go? Heaven may well be full of sweet music, but it doesn't enchant me. And then I ask myself how the Christian faith can inspire me, fascinate me, if I haven't already got the basis, the desire and longing for a next world, for survival after death? How am I supposed to convince other people of a happiness I don't seek myself? I object to God trying to force his happiness on to me, forcing me into a choice between all or nothing, between heaven and hell. I wasn't asked if I wanted to come into the world. Why can't I leave it again in peace?

It's the "next world". It has no appeal, and that naturally has an effect on this world. Why believe at all? The next world is a long way off (still)—and that doesn't necessarily depend on age. And here, in ordinary life, where the ordinary events and trivia trundle on, where one has one's job and one's responsibilities to cope with, where happiness and unhappiness, joy and sorrow, life and death are all under one roof and Sisyphus' boulder has to be rolled anew every day—what do you really get out of the Christian faith? I hardly ever pray. I don't know what meditation is. Sunday mass bores me. Sermons often make me want to scream, and I regard grace before meals as a lie. These are all symptoms, as doctors would say, symptoms of a disease that lies deeper. But what is the name of this disease? To my mind, the Christian faith no longer proves itself in practice. It no longer has a goal with which people today want to identify or for which—here and now—it would be worth giving one's life. For a Christian it may be some slight consolation to know that in this respect Christianity is in exactly the same position as other world-views. What should I be particularly concerned about as a Christian? How is a Christian any better off than his unbelieving neighbour? Are Christians inwardly happier, more content, more comforted than non-Christians? Even if they were (and with all the necessary reservations about unexamined generalisations!), subjective feeling on their own wouldn't seem to me to have too much weight. It would still leave unanswered the question what recipe the Christian faith has at hand for a better world today and tomorrow, and what is distinctively Christian about this recipe.

Szczesny writes somewhere: "What every human being, under whatever conditions, has to endure from his or her own unaided resources, what cannot be changed or avoided, these are the fundamental determinants of his or her existence. Human beings experience themselves as incompletely equipped and contradictorily endowed creatures. Their lives are limited. They are threatened by age and disease, accidents and disappointments. They fail to solve private and social problems and fail in their attempts to get to the bottom of things, and in the end they cannot say what the origin or meaning of this life is from which they will be removed with as little choice as when they entered it". If Christianity today constantly stresses that it is not trying to console people with the prospect of a better life in the next world, what does the faith have to offer those who want to work for a better life in this world? I don't share the view of those who accuse people today, and especially the younger generation, of a lack of readiness for self-denial and sacrifice (while themselves being quite happy to shuffle comfortably through life!). I also refuse to join the chorus of those who accuse young people of lack of idealism. As a fact, as a bare datum, it may be all true. But that isn't young people's fault. They have no idealism because there are no more ideals. They refuse to make sacrifices where the meaning and the goal to be achieved are no longer clear. So back to the question: What specific ideals has the Christian faith got to offer? What does Christian commitment in today's world look like?

I know that the answer to these questions cannot be found in a few sentences. But if we keep on putting off this question about the why of faith, if we go on putting up with being totally unable to say where the fire is that ought to be burning, and how I would be poorer if I hung my Christian faith up behind the door, then our churches will soon be even emptier, then commitment to ideals—and in the long run human beings need this—will take place in complete isolation from the Christian faith. Then the secular messiahs will get even bigger crowds and the charlatans of transcendence even more money. The Christian faith as a proclamation and an appeal must once again get through to the levels in a human being where there is a longing. But what does the man or woman of today want? Where are these hidden wishes whose fulfilment is the Christian faith? And where is the question to which the only answer is Jesus of Nazareth? Milan Machovec: "Why has Marx won millions of followers? Certainly not because he *didn't* believe in something, but above all because he had something positive to say to people, primarily about the quite ordinary situation of daily life, about the problems of work, the elimination of exploitation and oppression. But not just that: he also gave people a great ideal, the ideal of the human future". Where does the Christian faith say anything about the "ordinary situation of daily life"? Where is the "great ideal"?

* * *

Even the first enquiry, which covers just a couple of pages, contains more questions than can be answered in the whole book. What can one reply to this first question? I admit to a slight despair. Does this feeling—naturally unadmitted and repressed—derive from the same resigned scepticism and the absence of a real enthusiasm and hope which the enquiry finds in the modern generation? Ought I not to ask myself whether this is the reason why it is difficult for me to attempt an answer? Ought I not to ask myself whether it would not be more honest to let myself slip into the same sceptical resignation than to admit that I don't know an answer or that I'm too tired to try and work one out? And yet, why do I not do this? Are the only obstacles those which have nothing to do with sober logic or existential honesty? The old habits of a life which won't any longer come off the track it's travelled a thousand times? The pressure of a Christian common sense in society which still exists? Sheer fear that I still haven't plumbed the depths of the consequences of such a capitulation and yet cannot simply and confidently assure myself that I would, after all, be able to live a harmless superficial existence in spite of all the sceptical resignation, as the majority of my contemporaries do? In fact, they're neither radically Christian nor radically atheist, but to be precise and honest about it, they avoid a clear decision. I can't help feeling that in the end people don't take resigned scepticism quite seriously, but as well as this valium of life, they need other pills (pleasure, work, success, holidays and so on) to get by, but without being able to say seriously to themselves why they really want to get by. So when I ask myself why I don't simply surrender to this tired scepticism, although it does exist in me and I don't regard myself as a strong, unshakeable, religious hero, I do think that I have a different and deeper reason than the ones we have mentioned and one which I can freely draw on. In saying this, I'm not quite sure whether the first enquiry is one from a person who finds to his or her annoyance that faith in God and eternal life is difficult, or one from a person who, because such realities no longer appear in the area of his or her real life, has firmly given them up. But perhaps the enquirer will say that even he or she doesn't really know, and that this is indeed part of the resigned scepticism which no longer offers in any direction really clear choices which inspire enthusiasm.

I can't possibly try to answer all the points touched on in the enquiry. Nevertheless there is one point I do want to make because I don't accept the position of sceptical resignation, though of course it does threaten me, inwardly and outwardly. There is of course a prior question, whether one can claim the right or the duty to rely on sober arguments to answer a vague mood such as the one so vividly described in the enquiry. Can or must one oppose and resist such a mood even when one can't simply drive it away with a powerful word of rational control from one's inner being? Even though I don't believe that human beings can live by rational calculation alone, even though I know that the real and total life of a human being is fed by springs which come from hidden depths, nevertheless I'm firmly convinced, even in my own case, that not just everything which comes from this sort of inner mood is *ipso facto* valid and must be accepted. No, I'm also responsible even for my inner mood and rational reflection is one way of exercising this responsibility, even though this alone is not sufficient to give a responsible form to my mood. When I read some of the things in the first enquiry in the light of this conviction, they certainly seem to me to give a correct description of an actual mood in the enquirer and in myself, but at the same time to make the incorrect assumption that this mood is a hard fact in relation to which the only permissible question is whether one honestly admits it, not something for which one is responsible, which itself can be transformed again or at least be placed in a totally different perspective which changes everything. When I here and now feel no particular longing in myself for an eternal life, what follows from this? Is it absolutely certain that such a longing is lost to me absolutely and forever? Is it certain that in this regard I can't do anything except wait passively and in resignation in case such a longing one day comes over me? Or is there a point at some deeper level of my free existence at which I am in fact responsible for the presence or absence of this longing and must sort out by means of rational argument the direction in which I have to guide my subjectivity? None of that would be necessary, and this wouldn't have to be said, if my inner mood was so clear, so fixed and so infallible that there was absolutely nothing to be done about it except simply surrender to it, or if the responsible person possessed some other obvious means and criteria for guiding this inner mood apart from reflection. In short, is the lack of fascination of the Christian faith an argument against it or against me? That is a question which at least can't be swiftly dismissed. When people come along and say that Beethoven's music does absolutely nothing for them, you don't say to them: "Yes, you're quite right".

Is it possible for a person to be really indifferent to eternal life? This question is very complex. On the one hand one could say that it is impossible and unnecessary to be interested in the question of God's existence if one calmly expects the complete cessation of one's own existence. However, against this view one can argue that in the Old Testament, for example, a vital relationship to God which permeated the whole of life was achieved, although individuals did not expect a continuing life after death which would perfect them and make them happy, but only a shadowy existence without any power to structure their lives here and now. But this argument in turn is quite correctly refuted if one points out that if we honestly take seriously the idea that even existentially significant truths are part of a history which moves in one direction, then we do not have the right arbitrarily to go back to a point in the past of that history and position ourselves there because the naïveté of that past period simply no longer exists for us. On the other hand one could say that if the existence of God is in some way accepted, one can no longer seriously doubt the continued existence of a personal spiritual subject whom this God has, after all, called before his face. Or one can—and this is a third possibility—start from the belief, which one can demonstrate by argument, that in the long run a human being simply cannot avoid a longing for the definitiveness of his or her own existence, but that this means accepting with the same necessity the existence of what we call "God".

It is true that in the grey routine of our lives we can find little trace of a longing for eternal life. Like the things that take up our time, we too seem to escape into a grey indifference. But does such an everyday mood in which we even become indifferent to ourselves reveal the whole truth of our existence? No, reality is richer and deeper than the experience of the ordinary person on a bad day, and we have the duty to rescue the greater and deeper experiences for our everyday lives as far as we can, even if they're really (or apparently) only rarely given to us.

Suppose people have to make a difficult decision about the life of another person. May they say that according to physiological and sociological laws the decision is beyond their powers, that ultimately it is no more than the random conjunction of natural laws so that in the end it doesn't matter which way the decision goes, because either of the two possible decisions is the result of equally valid natural processes? When one is inside such a process of decision, can one really believe that all decisions are equally valid because all are in the same way naturally determined? When one is inside such a process of decision, can one really believe that all decisions are equally valid because all subsequently disappear without trace in the material and physiological machinery?

And even if someone does believe that such a view is compatible with and tenable within such a decision, that one can really shrug off one's own moral responsibility in the end, on to the automatic processes of physics and biology, can he or she then cheerfully say that this view too is no less the mere product of natural processes and not something for which we really have to take responsibility? Can people, while they're taking the decision, seriously think all the time that they really can in the end escape responsibility for the decision by creeping from the stage of genuinely personal history into the void in which there are no more responsible subjects?

The assumption that enduring and definitive free subjects exist is implicit in moral decisions. It makes no difference that people may be unaware of this, or that they shrink from this unavoidable assumption into a posteriori reflection because they begin to imagine this definitiveness as a sort of primitive extension in time made up of segments of time, and then can't take this as a serious hypothesis. Of course, time means the provisional. In such a world where everything is always provisional, in which everything which ever is topples into the void of what has been, decisions for which we take free responsibility cannot disappear; they cannot seek to escape into the void without contradicting their own nature. It may be difficult to "imagine" such timeless definitiveness. Nevertheless, today above all, when the real compatibility of what is expressed by different conceptual schemes can no longer be presented even in physics in a way which allows us to "imagine" it, we should be on our guard against lightly and angrily dismissing anything that can no longer be simply imagined as unreal or nonsense. If we do this we are only refusing to come to terms in thought and language with realities with which we are in fact engaged in the free exercise of responsibility.

Such an experience of being called to real definitiveness does not exist only in the case to which we have just been appealing. All personal operations of the mind and of freedom contain this claim to definitiveness, a claim which can only be denied from outside the actual operations. It would take us too long here to examine other similar personal operations to discover this assertion of definitiveness which is immanent in them.

Arguing in this way doesn't mean that I believe that such a process of argument is capable by itself of overcoming that *taedium vitae,* that bored lack of interest in eking out another day. Such arguments are no more than a serious question to the individual. They ask whether he or she is going to decide in favour of this boredom with life as the last word in his or her life. May not, they suggest, faith in the definitiveness of personal existence for "eternal life" prevail in a constantly renewed struggle full of a mixture of happiness and terror?

Of course there are many people—at least so it seems at first sight, but it is only at first sight—who live in an existential dizziness which seems quite normal and natural, in a twilight area between light and darkness. They believe they can and ought to live in a sceptical sobriety without making a final decision. However, this leaves the question open whether such "neutrality" is simply covering up the fact that one has secretly decided in favour of a final guilty resignation. It might be thought that this sort of situation is in fact not possible, that a human being must necessarily, in the ultimate depths of his or her existence, freely take hold of the yes which carries all these sceptical or angry no's and so ultimately cannot "be lost". But the Christian message of judgment and the two ways of attaining definitive existence, as blessed and as lost, and the genuinely radical difference in the possibilities of freedom warn us absolutely, on the basis of considerations which perhaps may be those of hope, against acquiring a certainty which would dissolve the burden of any decision of freedom in advance in a cheap optimism. And if the possibilities of rational argument in favour of "eternal life" are limited, even if such argument does not seek on its own to produce that life-giving conviction which illuminates and invigorates everything, nevertheless it has its own crucial significance. It obliges us to look for the other springs which must feed this hope.

People may not constantly try to escape from the seriousness and responsibility of their lives into the tasks of every day.

They may collect themselves, be still, silent, and so allow the unity and wholeness of their existence as such to appear. They may become aware that what has been entrusted to them is not just the thousand and one details of their busy lives, but their own selves; they may find the courage to reject, in anger, their own existential idleness. They may take care not to let the great moments of life go by, the moments in which truth is acknowledged to one's own disadvantage and love is done at the expense of one's own egotism. When they do this, they are uncovering the springs which feed the hope of eternal life, which cannot be generated by rational reflection alone.

When a person hears these arguments and remains passively in the dull indifference portrayed by the first enquiry, the "preacher" who put forward the argument can only ask himself whether he could not or ought not to have put the argument better, more clearly, more attractively and more forcefully, and keep on making renewed efforts to do it better. But the "preacher" must also keep on asking the hearer whether he or she is really going to continue passively in that dull resignation until a sacred fire from heaven consumes it. In this situation the "preacher" can only hope that history will go on and that the hearer will eventually come to the point where the "preacher" himself in overcoming his own resignation keeps on trying to make a stand.

Ought faith not to burn? That is the question. But ought we ourselves not to burn, we could ask in reply, and have we done our bit to make sure that we burn? Is it true that there is no difference at all between the details of the life of the believer and the unbeliever, but that faith is an ideological superstructure on top of a reality which is common to both? This question can't be answered with a straightforward yes or no. The enquiry presupposes that the question has to be answered empirically.

But how, in ordinary empirical reality, is one to distinguish believers from unbelievers? How are we to determine whether they differ in their lives or whether their "world-views" are ultimately of no importance for this life? Nor does it follow from what has just been said that the "theoretical" interpretations of human existence are of no importance for that existence simply because this existence in its unreflected reality and its interpretation are never simply identical, and can even be in contradiction without the contradiction being noticed. The correct interpretation of human existence is certainly an aid, and perhaps a crucial one, in the correct living-out of that existence, and a false or inadequate interpretation can be a mortal danger to the living-out of this existence.

To that extent, therefore, in spite of all the reservations just made, the question remains whether faith (as a conscious and verbalised "theory") has importance for real life, even when we ignore the argument that a theory is unavoidable and is in fact itself, in its way, part of life. In spite of everything, and indeed because of the difficulty just mentioned of empirically determining the effect on real life of belief and unbelief, it has to be said that the unbeliever and the believer live different lives.

First, no one, in practical life as opposed to arbitrary theory, can deny that theoretical considerations are not just secondary manifestations of a mental and social base, but also have an effect on this base. It may happen that someone puts a bullet through his brain in a despairing revulsion from life because he interprets his existence theoretically as meaningless. It makes no difference if one says this interpretation derives from a deeper basic position in which life is experienced as meaningless. Who can deny, without falling into a naturalistic determinism, that this pessimistic basic position (which we accept for the purposes of argument) inevitably resulted in such a pessimistic theory and, if this had not happened, the suicide too would not have taken place? Even a person like Stalin admitted in the end that the superstructure also had an effect on the base, a realisation which would have been meaningless and superfluous if this superstructure had in turn been the totally inescapable consequence of the base, so making the base itself ultimately the result of a deterministic cause or relationship. No, theory has an importance of its own, however difficult it may be to define or assess a human being in the core of his or her free personality simply in terms of his or her theory.

Again, if someone shows me an unbeliever who, not only in

the business of getting through her physiological existence, but also in the dimensions of love, loyalty, commitment to truth and so on, lives in a way that a believer could not better, then in my terms that person is, in the unreflected core of her existence, a believer and her theoretical superstructure contradicts—and this is possible for a variety of reasons—her actual faith. Here we should not forget that people these days are only too happy to disparage certain values and exclude them in advance from the standards for the moral assessment of a person with the result that in such a comparison a believer and an unbeliever no longer show any difference.

Again, on these assumptions it is simply not true that there is no visible difference between the life of a believer who has courageously chosen an ultimate absolute meaning for his life and so chosen eternal life and the ultimate unconditioned ground of that life, which we call God, and constantly renews that choice, and the life of a person who firmly rejects all this and goes on to draw real consequences for the conduct of his life. If the second person were still to live like the first, he would be—happily—simply inconsistent, whatever the particular reasons for this inconsistency might be. If this person angrily insists that he naturally respects the moral norms of life just as unconditionally as the first, then, on my terms, if his statement is true and radical in intention, he is a believer who is unable to analyse the implications of his own principles of conduct, or he has not yet reached the point in his life history at which his theoretical interpretation of human existence is forced to submit to an ultimate radical test of its strength. But wherever and whenever both, the theoretical believer and the theoretical unbeliever, take their interpretations of existence really radically and put them into practice in their lives consistently, to the last detail, then the lives they lead are quite plainly different.

One basic idea runs, explicitly or implicitly, through the whole of the first enquiry. Relativistic scepticism derives its claim to legitimacy from the enormous variety of religions, philosophies, and theoretical and practical interpretations of life. Naturally one can't automatically regard oneself as more clever, more honest or having a greater sense of responsibility than other people (at least in their majority); how then can I suppose that I in particular have had the good fortune, out of the many world-views on offer, to pick out the only right one? After all, isn't it usually just the one a person has inherited, and doesn't it appear natural only as long as one is securely fitted into the social milieu which corresponds to this particular world-view? Now it is of course true that we have a more difficult time with our personal convictions today than in previous ages when individuals were relieved of the burden of a personal decision by the ideology of a homogeneous society. But it is impossible to avoid the burden of this decision by escaping into a weary relativism; for this relativism too is only one of many world-views, not the avoidance of one, and, like all the others, it must face the question why it in particular, as opposed to all the others, is the right one.

Relativism as a theory which claims to be the only true system refutes itself because the denial of all absolutes cannot itself set itself up as absolute. But if the sceptic says that she lives sceptically but does not hold an absolute theory of scepticism, she can then be asked whether this statement is not in fact itself a theory in germ (and a theory which in turn refutes itself) and whether she can avoid giving others—and above all herself— even this account, a position which is simply impossible to the extent that a person cannot live totally in a dull refusal to think.

Within the Christian understanding of existence as a whole, it can and must be made clear that where Christianity has a correct understanding of itself it cannot possibly regard itself as one of many philosophical alternatives set out in a row for the human being to choose from. Anyone who really understands Christianity correctly cannot see any alternative alongside it. Christianity doesn't merely say this or that in a whole collection of individual propositions to each of which there is always a conceivable alternative. Christianity really says only one thing: that the infinite incomprehensibility which we call God exists, that we submit to it unconditionally as our own perfection, and that the acceptance of this submission has received a historical and unconditional guarantee in Jesus.

In comparison with this anything else in Christianity, how-ever important it may be, is secondary. But to this statement there are in fact no other alternative propositions which could refute it. All other propositions are, in contrast to this one, unimportant and they are simply the observation that human beings think (in each particular theoretical self-interpretation) that they are unable to perform this supreme act. Nevertheless such observations are no proof that persons cannot or should not make this supreme venture.

Persons who make this venture are convinced that all others around them, wherever pure evil is not being freely done, are accomplishing this supreme act in their lives, even if they can-not formulate for themselves, even in their theoretical reflec-tion, the glory of this act and so think that they're nothing more than human beings who can find no escape from the prison of a tired relativism. Those who make the venture experience this prison; they may experience it as inescapable. And yet, in ven-turing they find that they have already put a distance between themselves and their prison; they cannot, after all, just accept this imprisonment as natural. And when they try to put up with this prison which they cannot deny, in their apparent tired scepticism and hopeless resignation, and order themselves to feel this state as normal, their own resignation constantly pushes them towards the other alternative: the hope that does not give up, the hope for the light without at least a suspicion of which it would be impossible to experience darkness as dark-ness.

Such persons perhaps do not even know themselves whether in the deepest region of existence they have given up or still hope; they are angry with themselves that they are still bother-ing themselves and torturing themselves with such questions, and constantly try to use everyday duties and everyday plea-sures to run away from this ultimate question. It is possible for people to keep the front of the stage of their lives clear of the question whether in ultimate questions they are in despair or have hope. At least long enough for it to be impossible to ask them what they are ultimately doing. But always behind this stage, the stage upon which only what is feasible and what can be clearly stated is allowed to perform, sits the director of the whole play, the same person. Does he hope or has he despaired? In the long run and for the whole of existence there is here only one either/or and no position that could really dispense us from a choice. It is some progress if this choice is acted out in the full glare of the lights at the front of the stage of our lives.

Two

A certain faith?

The lack of appeal of the Christian religion, which I described in my first enquiry, and the fact that it has lost its power to motivate, has probably to do with the fact that religion as a mode of knowledge no longer carries the conviction it used to have. As a believer I do not know where my faith is leading me. Does it lead to knowledge of the truth? Or is religion the better probability? Or is religion nothing more than the expression of subjective conviction? Is it a personal certainty, many of which exist in the world, which, however, does not guarantee the truth of the beliefs? What Pius IX says about Christian religion may do nothing more than force an anguished smile from people of our time: "Nothing is more secure than our faith, there is nothing more definite, nothing more sacred, nothing which could rest upon a firmer basis". Is that really true? I would rather support Freud who associates faith with wishes. Freud says in *The Future of an Illusion*: "It would certainly be nice, if God as a creator of the world and as a 'kindly providence' existed as a moral world-order, a life after death; yet it is very striking that everything seems to be as we have to wish it".

I certainly do not want to be considered as a follower of Freud, at least not when he talks about the origin of religion. If one tries to meet the arguments of critics of religion, however, one is confronted with questions and problems one would not think of on one's own. Once you have fallen into the water you are wet. Is it not indeed strange that religion coincides so closely with the wishes of human beings? At this point we become afraid. Fear is something unpleasant. The fears of our time are probably different from those of former generations. But they are still there—the fear of life, of tomorrow, of an uncertain future of which we do not know what it holds for us. And then we are told not to be afraid. Then we want to be happy. Not only today. Not only sometimes. Without being able to say what it is, we want happiness. Happiness, however, is not attainable in this world. Like a child trying to run towards a rainbow without ever reaching it, we run after what we call happiness, without ever really catching it or ever being totally satisfied. And religion tells us that happiness is waiting for us. Not here, of course, but in the next life. Nobody likes to die. But there is eternal life. People suffer, starve, get old, and waste away. They are tortured and misused. But there is always "kindly providence" which knows what the point of all is and is guiding and controlling everything. Religion: wish or reality? A question. A thorn in the flesh of faith.

I would like to have the thorn pulled out. However, the question cannot be answered in that way. A wish, something which so remarkably corresponds to our demands and our longings, is for that very reason neither true nor false. It does not have to be true. It does not have to be false. Wishes can be fulfilled. They can also remain unfulfilled. The religious person would change the word "wish" into "hope". He or she would say that his or her hope is justified by faith. But what does faith then do? Where does it lead? What does it prove? If I am able to interpret the signs of the times correctly, it seems to me that believers today are not necessarily doomed to be ridiculous. The fact that there are people who believe is tolerated. It is not chic anymore to make fun of it; indeed people do not really argue about it. What is the point?

Yet, just this "tolerant" and benevolent indifference pushes the religious person into real abysses of insecurity, abysses in which you do not know whether the rope will hold or whether the bridges will carry you. Subjective integrity is assumed in the Pope as well as in the Dalai Lama, in the Christian as well as in the Bushman, in the Moslem as well as in the atheist. That is at least something, but is not enough to transform subjective integrity into objective truth. That is where we all are today. Rather perplexed. Perplexed before the innumerable signs which all indicate the same place and yet all point in different directions. And we admire the courage of those who definitely take one direction. But even they can only choose one way. Where does it lead? And what might be the reasons which make them take this particular direction? It is true: nobody can stand still. Out of necessity we choose some direction or another. Because human beings have to act and to live, because they have to organise and evaluate, they cannot stand around puzzling over signposts.

Now I can say to myself, I understand that I have to go, that I have to choose a direction. Yet how can I convince myself that the direction proposed by the Christian religion is the right one? If you have doubts sticking to your shoes it is difficult to walk. It is hard to live for probabilities. But can faith lead to more than greater or lesser probability? I want to explain my question, which still does not focus on the content of faith, but on the credibility of faith. I want to give reasons which seem to make religion—or, better, faith—dubious as a commitment to something one cannot know with the necessary certainty. People like to say today that doubts in faith are exciting, they somehow belong to religion. But how can one work for something which possibly exists, but is not known for sure?

What you said in your first answer I understand without any effort: No religion proves its truth in theory but in practice, in everyday life, in actions. Religion does not mean knowledge which does not have an effect on life. Someone can know all there is to know about Christianity, but at the same time be a long way from being a Christian (the opposite is also true). Faith needs action, commitment. One has to travel the road in order to know it. But there is a problem here. I cannot get rid of the suspicion that every commitment has an effect on the convictions of the believer. It seems that the greater the commitment the greater the readiness to believe. (In fact, this is not surprising. It is even natural, because something is "invested". And who would like to admit that he made a bad investment?) My conclusion from these thoughts is that everyone who lives their world-view with determination and commitment will find that this world-view proves true. I was brought up as a Christian. I do not know any other belief or any other religion—I mean from the inside, from having lived it—than the Christian one. But what would have happened if I had been born into a different world, into a society with different convictions and a different truth? Would I then not believe in something different, believe in it with the same naturalness and the same doubts I have as a Christian?

This suspicion is reinforced even more by an awareness of the social determination of religion. What sociologists of knowledge have found out may not be new. But still the believer cannot just ignore it. At least I cannot. What is it about? The sociology of knowledge tries to answer the question how a certain type of knowledge within a certain society comes into existence, is preserved and passed on. And it comes to the conclusion that in each case the convictions are held not because of their truth, but because of the "structures of plausibility" and "mechanisms of support" operating within a society. The American sociologist P.L. Berger says in his book *A Rumor of Angels:*

> One of the fundamental propositions of the sociology of knowledge is that the plausibility, in the sense of what people actually find credible, of views of reality depends upon the social support these receive. . . . Each plausibility structure can be further analysed in terms of its constituent elements—the specific human beings that "inhabit" it, the conversational network by which these "inhabitants" keep the reality in question going, the therapeutic practices and rituals, and the legitimations that go with them. For example, the maintenance of the Catholic faith in the consciousness of the individual requires that he maintain his relationship to the plausibility structure of Catholicism. This is, above all, a community of Catholics in his social milieu who continually support this faith. It will be useful if those who are of the greatest emotional significance to the individual (the ones whom George Herbert Mead called significant others) belong to this supportive community—it does not matter much if, say, the individual's dentist is a non-Catholic, but his wife and his closest personal friends had better be.

This really says everything. Yet, does not religion then turn out to be an entity dependent on social factors, whose content is no more credible than the mechanisms which support it? This means: it is not the content of religion which proves religion to be true, but, to put it crudely, its paraphernalia. Have I as a Christian any reason to see my belief in any other way? Does my religion attain an objective reality and pure truth or does it only seem plausible to me, because of the way I was brought up and because I am living in the corresponding structure of plausibility? Do I have no hope, in other words, of finding the truth in religion, but travel only one road (on which others travel with me), a road which is no better than any other?

What is faith? It is certainly not knowledge in the strict sense of the word. Yet how am I to make sure? How can I get to the point where I can say: Your faith is true, your faith is the true faith? Many Christians of today find it an enormous problem that many different religions exist. Although the specific beliefs are different, the structures and the motives show a horrible similarity in the most diverse beliefs. Everyone is, of course, convinced that his or her own faith is compelling and that it is really the true faith for everyone. In the age of pluralism in which (in Gehlen's words) people are confronted with a vast array of catechisms, the impression cannot be avoided that the subjective convictions of believers in the end do not reflect the truth of what is believed, but are influenced by different individual and social circumstances. Indeed, there seems to be no valid criterion for distinguishing different beliefs. The reason is that the subjective certainty which, for instance, Christians can claim in their religion can also be claimed in the same way by other religions or world-views. And therefore I ask myself: Where can certainty in religion come from? What can religion achieve as a way of discovering truth? How is the Christian religion more than a subjective conviction by which—I willingly admit—one can live a good and decent life, but which, on the other hand, does not guarantee the truth of what is believed? What is truth and how can I reach it, when it is associated with religion?

*   *   *

The second enquiry is still very closely related to the first, measured against the range of Christian doctrines. The critical question, when looked at closely, that is, whether any certainty of Christian faith exists at all, derives its doubts from reflections which, in the first enquiry caused a certain scepticism about any possibility of faith. It is therefore not surprising that the answer to the second question is not clearly distinct from the first. That does not matter, since we are confronted with a topic which in many apologias for the Christian religion is not made explicit enough, especially because traditional epistemology in Catholic Christianity is only slowly beginning to look honestly at the problems which, in the first two enquiries, are presented with such clarity. Because of this there can be no fundamental objection to returning to a previous point. Already in the first answer it was mentioned that Christianity cannot allow itself to be placed alongside other world-views which have been offered in the history of religion and are still offered in the public marketplace. In the first answer this remark was linked with the statement that the impossibility of comparing Christianity first of all has to be proved by what was to be said about the Christian religion and Christian faith later. Nevertheless, it turns out that the first answer has to be interpreted as part of the answer to the second enquiry.

The second enquiry calls the certainty of the Christian belief into question by the remark that this belief is created by wishes, a hope, but that such hopeful wishing is a doubtful business, which cannot produce and guarantee a certainty in faith. Let us leave open the question of whether faith is only a wish, while perhaps existing as a phenomenon which cannot be proved directly and empirically and providing the solution to all the problems which are otherwise left unanswered in our lives, or whether this faith has other sources of knowledge which cannot just be traced to wishes. Let us simply assume that faith is a wish for the existence of a reality by which the riddles of our existence are solved and the ultimate demands of our lives are fulfilled.

Having made this concession, which we are under no real obligation to make, we ask, whether the "wish" which supports the Christian religion, automatically makes it legitimate to doubt its object. Naturally, there are wishes whose existence does not guarantee the existence of their objects. I may wish to live to a hundred and still die at eighty. But is that true of every "wish"? Do all wishes, of whatever kind, belong to the single category of wishes whose fulfilment is not guaranteed?

The second enquiry always talks hesitantly and doubtfully about "certainty" in faith and in doing so always comes back to the question of the truth of faith: Is it certain that the Christian religion is true? For the moment we do not want to get involved in the difficult epistemological question of how the truth and certainty of a conviction have to be distinguished and yet are closely connected. The only thing we are interested in here is the realisation that there are certainties which can be doubted and that a person simply cannot live without them, and also that such (doubted) certainties are always supported by a personal decision in favour of them, but that this is no argument against the real certainty and truth of the beliefs concerned. That, for example, selfless love makes sense, can only be discovered in choosing it. This does not mean that the meaningfulness of such love is a subjective invention which one can just as well do without.

In the realm of existence there are realities which can be discovered to be real, "true" and "certain" only in being chosen. As long as somebody refuses this free agreement to this reality and can only talk theoretically about it, he or she will be blind to it. It can be proved, however, that there necessarily exist realities which can only show themselves as they really are when we entrust ourselves to them. We therefore cannot say that this or that is non-existent or that its existence is doubtful, because it does not impose its existence on us against our reluctance. The believer and the unbeliever must not demand a certainty of faith, which would be independent of such a free surrender to the reality of faith. There is, of course, no such faith. It cannot exist, because the reality which it offers does not really mean a particular item of reality, but the whole of reality in general and of human existence; and this whole naturally cannot be aimed at and defined from a point outside of itself.

Regarding the certainty of faith, which derives from the nature of faith as a trusting and open relationship to the whole of reality, as subjective does not make faith and unbelief equally valid possibilities between which we can just choose. A free rejection of a positive attitude of trust in reality is in general the result of a secret acceptance which is prior to freedom, and so the unbeliever (in this general sense of an ultimate basic attitude) is caught in an insoluble contradiction with himself.

For the moment, it is only important to accept that freedom and certainty in matters of faith do not contradict each other, provided that the believer understands that no certainty can be expected which would be independent of such a decision of freedom. Where freedom admits courageously the whole of reality even in its incomprehensibility it has the light of its certainty in itself, even though it cannot take it to the further point of making this preliminary act of trust in an ultimate and all-embracing meaning of reality. The question can be at most, how to bring persons who think they are living without hope in such sceptical doubt to such an affirmation of ultimate trust. Of course, such a free certainty cannot be taught. It can only be pointed out to people that their sceptical reserve, because everything seems to lack ultimate certainty, still lives in its secret depths by an implicit acceptance which has to be appropriated in freedom. Even such sceptical reserve still comes from an implicit assumption of a distinction between truth and error, good and bad, above and below. If this were not so, there would be no possibility of an explanation of sceptical neutrality.

The statement that no clear distinction is possible is again the statement that things do not simply merge arbitrarily. It is an expression of pain at an inability, which would be completely inconceivable if indeterminacy and uncertainty had the last word. Darkness can only be perceived by an eye which was created for light. The believer's essential optimism will make him or her say that in the life of every human being a particular situation will always arise which forces him or her to make a choice for a radical acceptance or a radical rejection, and in doing so emerge from this featureless greyness in which he or she thinks and lives.

Believers will even have the quiet hope that the result will in fact be an acceptance, because they cannot imagine a freedom, created by God, with all the inexorable radicality of a choice between two possibilities, in which an acceptance by freedom did not have a much greater chance than a rejection. In the end there is no neutrality, and an acceptance of reality comes more directly from God than a rejection. In reflecting on certainty in faith we have worked—and we have no wish to conceal this— with a concept of "faith" according to which faith is nothing other than the positive and unconditional acceptance of one's own existence as meaningful and open to a final fulfilment, which we call God. It must, of course, be shown later in more detail that such a belief is already the original seed of the Christian faith and, vice versa, that Christian faith is nothing but the pure and healthy development of this very seed.

However, since the second enquiry casts doubt on faith by means of a general and diffuse doubt of any certainty in any propositions of whatever kind, we must stress here that such a general scepticism which seems to be prior to any specific act of faith is really already unbelief, and that its opposite, the courage to accept absolutely that existence has meaning, is already faith.

The second enquiry casts doubt on the Christian faith by drawing attention to its social conditioning in the believer. It is obvious that such a social conditioning of faith in practice in a believer cannot be denied. Can I know that I or the pope would be Catholic Christians if we had not grown up in a Christian and Catholic environment and had not constantly sought instinctively those social supports which makes it easier to be a Catholic Christian? But what if we do honestly admit that (and, as is normal among Christians, interpret it as a grace of God)? Is there any set of beliefs or interpretation of existence which could claim to be totally independent of such social factors? Is not a radical rejection of and revolt against a dominant ideology in the social environment to which one originally belongs in part the product of that environment? One does not protest against every conceivable position, but only against the beliefs which exist in one's own environment, and one is therefore dependent on these and not on others.

Unless one holds the ultimately self-defeating view that all socially conditioned views are automatically equally valid because of this conditioning, and equally true or equally false, knowledge of the social conditioning cannot nullify or replace a search for truth. It must simply be treated as a call always to allow for the danger of prejudice deriving from one's own background when trying to determine truth. This is not to deny that in actual Christian apologetics throughout the centuries a great deal of such prejudice has been at work and has prevented difficulties from being clearly seen, with the result that we did not learn, or did not learn quickly enough, much of what our opponents had to teach us. It is a fact that if one is convinced of a proposition one very quickly finds arguments for it, even if they are in themselves bad, though this again is not to say that a proposition is necessarily false because bad arguments are used to defend it.

But even when all this is admitted, it must remain clear that social conditioning does not make the question of truth redundant. Nor does this social conditioning mean that the search for truth is hopeless, otherwise the phenomenon that people break with the ideology of their society and their origins would be inexplicable. Controversies on the level of rational argument have a retroactive effect on the attitudes produced by a particular society and historical situation. The individual's social situation is itself a historical entity in a process of change, to which the individual can and should contribute. When, in its New Testament period, Christianity found faith and martyrdom intimately linked, it believed strongly that faith had something to do with rejection of an ideology prevailing and accepted as obvious in a particular society. It believed that faith was precisely a break with such an ideology which defended itself so brutally, and indeed genuine faith only when it was prepared for such a break. This does not make such faith simply "apolitical"; it means that it retains historical and social assumptions which enable one to tell that it has particular historical and social origins. As a believer, one accepts these with good will and patience, and is not forced to make an absolute protest even against one's parents and the century one was born into. By its nature, the Christian faith is the overcoming of this historical conditioning and so of the relativity which attaches to any human system of thought from its situation. This faith is the event in which one is in contact with God himself, who holds together and supports all limitations, historical situations and conditioning. If we have and can have contact with this God in himself, we still remain rooted in a particular historical conditioning, but it is open (in faith, hope and love) to the incomprehensible God who is totally unconditioned. Of course we can only say this when we understand Christianity as something which does not simply consist of words and statements about something, but which contains the infinite reality of God as our possession. When we realise this, we must talk about it, even if our language remains infinitely far behind the reality our possession and experience of which it haltingly describes.

Once we accept the view that a human being is not in contact with God only by forming propositions about him in conscious awareness or receiving them through social indoctrination, the real and difficult question becomes why any "launching ramp" and any historical starting-point should not in principle be equally valid and appropriate for achieving that breakthrough to that intimate contact with the real God which surpasses all talk about him. The difficulty is this: it seems that at least all the religions which explicitly mention a God and distinguish him from us meet each other in this God and so become one. They then appear to differ only in the historical conditioning of their starting-points (the way the problem of God is posed, the conceptual system, the verbal and social expressions of the relationship with God). On the other hand, Christianity seems to regard only one historical starting-point and one social form as valid: Jesus Christ and the Church.

If therefore we say that Christianity is superior to historical relativism because it is really in contact with God himself, we seem not to have answered the historical scepticism of the second enquiry. We would have answered it or confirmed it (whichever one prefers) if all religions were concerned only with God himself and all historical starting-points were equally valid (at least in principle). But this seems to be ruled out by faith in Jesus Christ (and, deriving from that, in his Church). The whole problem is made more difficult by the fact that Catholic Christianity does not deny, but explicitly asserts, that a person may reach intimate union with God outside institutional Christianity if he or she knows nothing about Christ through no fault of his or her own.

Catholic Christianity seems here to be calling in question its own universal necessity for salvation. The question why Christianity has a universal and absolute character, not merely in its goal (God), but also in its starting-point, is therefore very difficult, even if the "absoluteness" of the starting point and that of the goal cannot be regarded as simply identical. Nevertheless, while we cannot here settle the whole problem of avoiding religious relativism, despite the multiplicity of religions, we can at least make one adequate statement: Jesus Christ, who was crucified and rose from the dead, is not just any religious phenomenon which provides a stimulus and starting-point for a relationship with God, even one infinitely superior to all religions, but the successful (resurrection!) event of the transition from finite individuality into the one, silent, incomprehensible infinity (death) which we call God. Because of this, there is no comparable religious phenomenon which could rival this one process or make it relative.

Christianity does not deny that there exist many initial starting-points (which relativise each other) for the basic process of religion, the opening of human beings towards God, a process supported by God himself. It merely says that all the religious phenomena which start in this way must pass through the same zero-point of death, and that the success of this transition has been guaranteed by the death of Jesus and has been made accessible to us in the experience of his resurrection. Inasmuch as all the prior diversity of religious experiences are starting-points for an identical final surrender of human beings to God in freedom, Christianity does not deny them but in principle regards them as valuable.

The only question is thus how Christianity in its actual ecclesial form can gradually and explicitly integrate into itself in the course of its history the various starting-points which still lie before the cross of Christ. How and why the individual human being who dies passes through the death of Christ as his salvation even if he or she has no explicit knowledge of him or, without any fault of his or her own, does not recognise Christ's significance for his or her salvation, is a question we do not have to answer here. When looked at more closely, the historical and social conditioning of Christianity, which at first sight seems to place it on the same level as many other religions, does not destroy its uniqueness and absoluteness, but is in fact the event by which all religions break out of their historical and social conditioning to achieve direct contact with God himself, in that in Jesus Christ this breakthrough is seen to have succeeded and to be experienced.

If all religions and world-views are not automatically subsumed under a vague, meaningless concept of "religion", but are examined to see what precisely they assert of themselves, the historical conditioning of Christianity or other religions and the resulting plurality of religions and systems is no reason to adopt religious scepticism. The historical and social conditioning of all religions has not just to be appreciated (though it must be), but recognised as something which can be transcended and has already ultimately been transcended in the death of Jesus.

To whom can this hope be denied? If it did not secretly exist, the pain of this relativism and pluralism could never be overcome. And if Christianity is precisely the acknowledgment of this hope and nothing else, it cannot let itself be included in a grey mass of equally valid religions and systems. A person may abandon this hope, or doubt that it has been finally confirmed by the victorious death of Jesus, but it cannot simply be included among the other world-views. To do so would be as ludicrous as to regard as consistent attitudes a recognition of the existence of absolute truth and a denial of such truth, when in fact the firm denial of such truth is itself a covert presupposition of it or has no specifiable meaning.

All that has just been said, and all that has to be said in answer to the second enquiry, can perhaps be illustrated by the following idea: we recognise, as the second enquiry said, that we have to choose one direction and cannot take all the conceivable and available directions. On the other hand, we doubt that the particular direction advocated by Christianity is the right one or leads to the goal, when there are so many other directions taken by so many other people. These doubts would have no meaning at all, and would be trivial, and all the directions would be only apparently different from one another, if we assumed that all of them or none of them led to the goal. In other words, underlying the doubt is a belief in the existence of one (or several) directions and of a goal. The doubt does not make it doubtful, but confirms it. One must choose a direction, and the statement that one stays at the crossroads, puzzled and despairing, because there are too many directions available which one cannot reconnoitre is itself the choice of one direction. What therefore if the direction we ourselves take were nothing but the belief that, provided that one travels honestly and faithfully (through no matter what stages), we arrive, not at just any goal, but at an infinity of reality and finality where there is no longer one thing or another, and which is called God?

This direction is not just one among many, but is *the* direction because it has automatically made a choice among directions redundant.

This one direction, which is *the* direction, is, however, Christianity, because it says nothing other than that human beings will eventually reach the incomprehensible infinity of God with which nothing is comparable, and that this fact is guaranteed and made accessible in Jesus Christ. All other experiences, interpretations of life, theories, and so on are, in comparison with this, merely secondary views on which agreement is unnecessary, or they are secondary conclusions from this single radical message of Christianity.

When someone holds this conviction, he is in a mental state in which all sceptical relativism has already been left behind. This is certainly not to say that relative phenomena do not exist, but that we are dealing with totality as such, and not just with the particular contents of this totality, which conflict and make each other relative. This direction which brings us to the totality naturally comes to be suspected of being only one of the many conceivable directions (none of which definitely leads to the goal) when and to the degree that it is given verbal expression and so placed alongside other systems as one of many. This appearance naturally always exists, and has constantly to be fought against, by going in one's own direction and not just talking about it, that is, by unconditionally but hopefully passing over all particular realities, goods, and goals to surrender to the incomprehensible mystery of our existence.

Of course one can always ask: How do I do that? How does a breakthrough really take place, through the thousand and one fragmented details of our lives and our world to the original unity of this reality? It is clear that this direct encounter with the original reality called God does not in fact take place where this unity and our relationship to it are expressed conceptually; the resulting verbal images (which easily become idols) submerge the reality under a mass of detail. This real event, which in itself is no longer threatened by sceptical relativism, takes place in its purest form where a human being, exercising an ultimate freedom, transcends the plurality of reality (of which he or she is also a part in his or her finite reality) in a hope and selfless love which does not in any way derive its legitimacy from this plural reality as such. It takes place where a final hope is set against all hope and love leads the human being into a silent infinity, out of the prison of his or her own egotism to which there is no return.

It can of course be objected that such an encounter of a particular finite subject with the one infinite totality is not possible—by definition—because the particular can have no contact with the totality without particularising the totality or making itself the totality. But if we remember that such language, which derives from quantity, may not be pressed, we may say that I, as an individual and finite creature, can have contact with the original, infinite totality which unites everything because I in fact have contact with it in unconditional hope and love. That in this process the totality itself must make a still earlier approach to me, and support my approach to it with itself, is natural (and is explicitly and separately stated in the Christian doctrine of grace).

Have we now said how this feat of achieving the only means of overcoming sceptical relativism and the fear of not having certainty is accomplished? Yes, if we understand what it was that had to be said. No, because what was said can be understood only by being performed. This of course raises the old question, which we have touched on before, of how people can be called on to do something which is at the same time said to be understood only in being done. This dilemma can be resolved only by the assumption that in every human being, what they will do in freedom is already irresistibly present, as an offer and to some degree as a rehearsal, and that therefore the act of freedom, in which the legitimation of the action is first expressed, is not a purely random act.

Freedom is never experienced as an incomprehensible explosion, something which suddenly starts from zero, but as something which has always already become active by the time conscious reflection begins. A person has always already hoped and loved, at least rudimentarily and in bursts; a person has always tasted, at least in minute quantity, the meaningfulness of hope and love as opposed to despair and egotism. A dawn of promise, whether we like it or not, has always already lightened the dark sky over our lives. But we must (and no force can make us) freely allow this hope and love which we have already experienced, this hope and love which, as we can say in Christian language, God's providence has always already gently coaxed out of creaturely freedom, to have its full and final scope through all the new turns taken by our life. This will give us the experience of that certainty which cannot be produced merely by rational debate, and which is at the heart of the act of unconditional hope and love.

Three

Does God exist?

Where the question of God is concerned, I find myself in a curious situation. At one time I find the existence of God utterly obvious, since without it nothing makes sense, from the wonders of "nature" to my own sense of myself and to the place where "the heart has its reasons". Again at another time the existence of the reality called "God" seems to me so senseless that I would like to throw in the towel. Which only goes to show that the religious sense too is affected by moods. Wilhelm Raabe writes somewhere: "It is a mistake or a downright lie to claim that when a person is unhappy or overwhelmed by distress and worry, a beautiful place and a wonderful view will bring them relief. It is simply not true, quite the opposite, nothing is worse for someone distressed or sorrowing than a broad sunlit panorama seen from a mountain top glowing with all the sweet colours of the earth. It is too bad, and indeed frightening, but it is true: in a gloomy mood one enjoys storm and rain and feels the beauty of nature as a slap in the face, an insult, and begins to hate all the seven days of creation".

What am I trying to say? I am simply trying to point out that there are moods in which the misery of the world, the grind and the toil, the suffering and the hopelessness, are quite capable of producing a state of mind in which the "glorious view" which is "God" seems more like an insult than a consolation. Without God the equation of a human life does not work out. But does it work out with God? *De humoribus non disputandum.* And so I ask myself why, after all, I am one of those who do not want to commit themselves to one side or the other. Who do not know themselves whether they are supposed to believe in God or not. Who would like to believe if only they could, and say to themselves that we will all know in the end, when we have closed our eyes forever.

But my doubts about the existence of God honestly do not just depend on moods. So what about the arguments which support the existence of God? I want—no, I must—examine them. I must see whether the bridges hold up or whether they crash into the void when you try to walk on them, into the deepest possible void since this void would be the most appalling deception. For a start, there are two problems I keep coming back to. Anyone who offers a proof for the existence of God—or perhaps it is better to say anyone who wants to prove the existence of God—necessarily starts from the assumption that, for everything that exists, there must be a sufficient reason, a reason that explains the data. The "data" may be the world as a whole, but they may also be my personal experiences, which constantly push out beyond the world, seek more than the world can offer, and can never stop. Experiences of happiness in this world seem in some way to be no more than the glimmering of a happiness which would be totally satisfying. They seem to be the promise and prediction of a bliss which is not of this world, cannot be of this world. And yet, I cannot get rid of the idea that all this searching for a reason for what I am and for what I cannot help hoping, that the pressure to find an answer and a reason need not in fact be anything more than an extremely subjective matter. Is it not possible that the human "instinctive search for meaning" exists only because human beings are "built" in this way and therefore search, have to search, where there is nothing to find? Claude Lévi-Strauss says precisely this: "Personally, I don't come up against the question of God. I find it completely tolerable to pass my life knowing that I will never be able to explain the totality of the universe". I take this statement as meaning that Lévi-Strauss—with many others—is happy to let believers keep their faith, but himself prefers to let the questions stop when the answer to be expected no longer has any meaning.

And that leads me to the second point in this line of thought. The believer accuses the person without faith of stopping his or her questioning too soon, of giving up too early in the search for an adequate explanation. And it is true that those who think like Lévi-Strauss must sometime stop asking questions. They must, at some point, be satisfied, accept themselves and the world as they in fact are, and make the best of it.

But why? Ultimately the belief that "God" is the answer to the thousand and one questions of human life is not in fact an answer. God becomes a sort of juggling-trick. His existence is asserted so that everything that we find puzzling, inexplicable, and unintelligible can be pushed off into the great unknown. Human questioning has to come to an end, not just because one person has not time enough and there are other things to do, but mainly because a point is reached at which what is, the fact world if you like, simply has to be accepted. For believers, God is a "fact" of this sort—where he comes from, why he exists at all, why he is the highest value of our life, the meaning of our existence, love in person who has his adequate explanation "in himself"—all these are supposed to be facts it makes no sense to question. God simply is like this. He is like this by our definition.

But if this is so, is there really any important distinction between religion and atheism? Since human beings must stop asking questions somewhere, does it matter where they in fact stop? Or, to put it another way, is it not more honest to let questioning stop where the limits are still recognisable? Ought we not to leave the inexplicable as it is without taking refuge in a reality which is so "totally other" that we can no longer have any idea of it? The believer has to make his assertion about God, but have I not just as much right to accept, not God, but the world as the ultimate inexplicable fact which "simply is"? Isn't God an "answer" only because he—to put it crudely—can do everything and also unites in himself the most contradictory things? But doesn't God then become a dump for all the questions to which we have no answer, a dump where we can toss anything, a place we desperately want? Freud said: "We tell ourselves it would be lovely if a God existed as the creator of the world and a kindly providence, a moral world order and a life after death, but it is very noticeable that all this is just the way we cannot help wishing it. And it would be even stranger if our poor, ignorant, unfree forefathers had succeeded in finding the solution to all these difficult riddles of the world". Is God only a wish which we are compelled to wish because we need a dump for all our questions and look for something like this because we are simply built in that way? In that case, wouldn't it be more honest to say that I will put up with my ignorance, put up with knowing that the infinite extent of our longings and wishes is not necessarily going to be filled? Are not people who believe in God in fact in the "infantile" stage in which wishes are taken for reality, simply unable to grow up and live in a world without illusions?

Within the limits of this question, it is not possible to bring in all the arguments of the atheist, nor is it necessary. For example, I—though perhaps many others disagree—find banal the arguments used in critical rationalism and other theories that God is an "empty formula", a word of which it is impossible to say what it is supposed to mean. At the most, for me, it raises the question of how much truth there is in what H. Albert has called the "immunisation strategy". In the concept "God", the argument runs, all possible ideas, even the most contradictory, may be combined, but there is every reason to doubt whether this combination of ideas in turn produces a meaningful and intelligible content. I want to focus this idea on just one point which makes me and others doubt the existence of God. I mean the co-existence of God's omnipotence and his goodness. I cannot forget the comment made by a friend of mine whose mother died in terrible suffering. Any doctor, he said, who was able to prevent such suffering and still did not would be condemned by a court. And God? In his play *Draussen vor der Tür*, evoking the horrors of the second world war (and, one is tempted to say, of all wars), Wolfgang Borchert makes a character put the counter-question to the God who—as we say—only "permits" all this, "Where were you really when the bombs were going off, dear God? Or were you 'dear' when my patrol lost eleven men? . . . The eleven men certainly shouted in the lonely wood, but you weren't there, just not there, dear God? Were you 'dear' in Stalingrad, dear God? . . . When were you really 'dear', dear God, when"? From Dostoyevsky to Simone Weil, this idea can be found in a thousand variations, and it goes back to the beginnings of any form of theism. The believer, as we already hinted, says that God only permits this, or that all suffering is the result of human sin and guilt. Be honest. Do you believe that? And, if not, doesn't the believer in God "immunise" his or her faith by means of all sorts of constructions, a sort of mental acrobatics? God only permits; God wants to test human beings; God knows the reason for all this. I am not so keen on going through all these mental acrobatics when the safety net of sound reason is missing. Wouldn't the world necessarily look different if God were really both all-good and all-powerful? That's what makes me doubtful. And, going on from what I have just said, I think that the world is in fact more intelligible if it runs its course without a kindly helmsman, if it follows its laws and human beings submit in quiet resignation without believing in the one who is in fact no answer.

One way or another, it seems to me, unless we are just going to sweep this idea under the carpet, that to believe in the existence of God is possible only with a generous portion of good will. Have those, have we, who believe in God, perhaps already made too great an investment to be able to turn back now? Or at least to leave the question open? To say we don't know? We don't know whether God exists? And we have made an investment! Parts of our lives, our energy and our self-denial. Are we still able to understand the atheist's arguments?

This brings me to a last idea. Everything so far was perhaps a little theoretical, moved on a level at which few people think, though I think that much of what we said is in the back of the minds of believers. I want now to ask you a personal question, and I hope that you will take it in the way that is obsesses me, and not as a reflection on the honesty of your faith in God. What I ask myself—and now I put this question to you—is what precisely would have to happen or be the case for you not to believe in God? Is your faith in God so firm that nothing at all can shake it? Can you imagine that a theoretical argument or an incident in your life might lead you to deny the existence of God? Not merely to doubt God with that uncertainty which belongs to faith, but to lose hope in God to such an extent that you denied his existence? The fact of loss of faith does exist, and persons who lose faith in God have their reasons even if they cannot give them adequate expression. Is your faith in God such that you could never abandon it no matter what arguments or vicissitudes you might be confronted with, perhaps will be confronted with? This is no longer a "theoretical" question. It would help many people to know what would have to happen or be the case for belief in God to be impossible. And, conversely, there would then be a criterion to justify faith in God—assuming that the case which forces us to deny God does not exist and does not occur.

* * *

It is only with fear and trembling that I attempt a few observations on the third enquiry. How else can one speak about the inconceivable mystery which we call God? It would be a mistake to think that it was possible to talk about God as one talks about the moon or a neutron. But how is one to talk about God in a language adequate to this unique reality, in language which is no more than the threshold of adoring silence? And how is one to speak about God to other persons when these persons do not so much want an exposition of what, at the root of their existence, they in fact already know, but instead are inclined, in irritation or disappointment, to ignore this basic experience because it does not always dominate their whole life in radiant clarity and power? Where is one to begin? What is one to discuss, and what is one to leave out; what should one try to say more accurately when one only has a couple of pages while the latest book considering the existence of God runs to a thousand pages? Should one try to argue with the latest subtleties of metaphysics? Should one appeal to the history of theism, which is basically identical with the history of the human race as such and, despite the worldwide spread of atheism, is still far from over? Or should one try a more down-to-earth approach and show from everyday experience that, without that incomprehensibility which we call God and which alone offers an infinite field of freedom, life is impossible and human beings suffocate in the narrow space in which they lock themselves because inside it everything is clear while the incomprehensibility of the mystery of God is unbearable? I don't know where to begin, so I shall limit myself to simply following the text of the third enquiry and making a remark here and there. At the same time I want to enter a formal protest that this should not be taken to imply that there is nothing better, nothing more precise, nothing more impressive that can be said about God than the few sentences which must serve as the answer to the third enquiry.

When I am asked, or ask myself, why I don't simply make this more impressive statement about God, if in fact it can be made, then I could put a counter-question: is the question itself not suspicious of precisely everything impressive and moving? Do I have to be able myself to describe the glory of a wonderful spring morning when I say I saw this morning and it was wonderful? Is it not obvious that the ultimate and all-embracing experience is the least capable of being expressed in words? Do not all words derive from particular experiences and particular realities or (if this is perhaps not quite correct) are they not exposed to the sceptical objection that they are poetry with no verifiable content? So we keep to our plan: I shall simply make a few observations as I follow the text of the third enquiry.

The third enquiry begins with a reference to "moods" which influence the conviction or doubt of the existence of God. We are told: *De humoribus non disputandum.* I have already tried to refute this in the answers to the first two enquiries. As I see it, attitudes, while very important realities, are not realities which automatically cannot be discussed, inaccessible to further enquiry and not requiring any legitimation. Even for our attitudes we are responsible. When we realise this, it is not so easy to get away with the claim that in a particular mood the idea of "God" seems more an insult than a consolation. Let us accept in good faith the accuracy of the claim, but is the attitude of being insulted legitimate? Must the idea of "God" always console us?

Isn't this demand already in itself a distortion of the idea of "God", which cannot be properly considered until it is freed from the net of our own needs? "Does the equation of a human life work out with God?" This is the question which comes out of this bleak mood. But does the equation in fact "work out" for us if it has to enter into the incomprehensibility of God, and it is only in this voluntary entry of the equation of our life into incomprehensibility that we can at all understand what is meant by God? Naturally one can say that there is nothing to be done with an incomprehensibility which one tolerates, and that real atheism consists in nothing other than the refusal to be bothered with God who is, by definition, incomprehensible. And yet, in the reality of human existence, can we remain indifferent to such an incomprehensibility when it stares us in the face on all sides? This alone shows that the attempt to be an atheist in one's life does not consist in the declaration that nothing like God exists, but is the assertion that one will not or cannot have anything to do with the one absolute totality which is at the root of all reality, when one is only a particle of that reality which cannot even take up an independent relation to the original unity preceding all multiplicity. Is it true that it is impossible to be concerned intellectually and freely with the mystery that, by definition, remains insoluble to all eternity, indeed works out by being insoluble, when we, as we Christians hope, have been brought into direct contact with it? That seems to me to be the real problem, not the "existence" of God for the denial of which there can, after all, be no positive reasons. But we shall have to keep coming back to this later. For the moment then just this: attitudes exist, they are significant, they also influence our actual relationship to God; however, they are no criterion by which a person who wants to be responsible can answer this substantive question.

The proof or "demonstration" of the existence of God starts, you say, from the assumption that everything must have a sufficient reason which "explains the data". This of course admits that these data which are to be explained may be both the "material" world as a whole and the personal subject with its needs and claims. At this point, however, we must ask whether in fact a modern "demonstration" of the existence of God does or must proceed in this way, whether the schema of the argument from an effect to a cause (thunder–lightning; egg–chicken) in the normal sense really gives us the structure of a modern proof of the existence of God. If it did, then certainly we could raise the question with which the third enquiry is concerned, the question at what point we are going to stop in such arguments (whether at the chicken or the egg), and why the obviousness of God, beyond which we cannot look to find a further reason, may not be regarded as an attribute of the world itself as a whole. (We should not forget that the traditional classical proofs of the existence of God also concern themselves with this question, and have a great deal to say, even if they traditionally present themselves as a search for an adequate reason for the existence of the world.)

However, I don't think that the modern demonstration of God's existence needs to be disturbed in any way by the question of the legitimacy of a pattern of thought which goes from an effect to a cause. This pattern of course presupposes that in the process of thought one first comes to "world" or "subject" and then, in a totally separate enquiry looks for a sufficient reason for the existence of something that was first encountered simply in the obviousness of its existence. This appears to be a new enquiry which one is quite free to omit. But what if this pattern which is implicitly assumed to be obvious does not at all reflect the peculiarity of the demonstration of the existence of God if this demonstration is properly understood? What if the implicit and unanalysed intuition of what we call God were the condition of the possibility of our knowledge of the world as such and of the subject, and so the sequence which the question assumes as obvious in our knowledge did not exist at all? What if the sequence was simply the sequence of what was known explicitly and in verbal objectivation, but not the "atemporal" succession of the condition of the possibility of knowledge and the knowledge itself?

What—to put it another way and more precisely—if the particular realities of the world and of subjects always and everywhere confronted human beings in an open, though not explicit (known about, but not understood) clarity of consciousness with an unlimited horizon? What if the intuition of this infinite expanse always told us what was meant by God and this pointer to God could in no way be abolished because it is the condition of the possibility of any sort of knowledge? This might be true even if this conscious condition of the possibility of any sort of knowledge were not translated into object consciousness as something known, and this condition of possibility could be irresistibly established even where it was consciously denied in an act of knowledge.

All this is simply intended to point out that the model of a demonstration of the existence of God which the third enquiry assumes as obvious can in no way be taken for granted. It is impossible to call a halt at an arbitrary point on the journey of the spiritual subject because it is always possible that one is no longer in fact at the point at which one thinks one is, and that one is incorrectly interpreting—through innocent error or culpably—one's true position (which is given by the subject's own spiritual structure and by his or her free acceptance of this).

When the third enquiry says that people like Lévi-Strauss stopped asking questions where the answers to be expected no longer produced any meaning, I would like to know how Lévi-Strauss knew that in advance. What such people are really doing is not abandoning a question before it has been raised or answered; they pose a question and answer it with a statement that it has been given an incorrect answer by others. This statement, however, is also an answer, even if a bad one. Once again, it amounts basically to saying that one should not try to concern oneself with the elusive mystery which surrounds all human knowledge and which one comes up against when one considers the ultimate structure of knowledge and freedom which lead into the incomprehensible.

But precisely at this point knowledge and freedom enter a region of inexpressible terror, when they begin to consider their own incomprehensibility in this way and no longer employ themselves unthinkingly as instruments for dealing with the various objects which fill our everyday life. At least a Christian has the courage (which he experiences completely as a gift) to address this incomprehensibility in itself and to accept it lovingly as the content of his own perfection, this incomprehensibility from which the atheist and the sceptic turn away with a shudder. And, in the individual case, even a believing Christian does not know whether this turning away, in horror, irritation, or discouragement, is a mysterious form of recognition of God or a sin which, as long as it exists, cannot be forgiven.

We now come to the second point of the third enquiry, the intellectual difficulties about the existence of God. The essence of this "second point" seems to me to be contained in the remark that God, as the incomprehensible, the one about whom, by definition, no more questions can be asked, and who must therefore simply be accepted, really explains nothing. There is in the end, it implies, no difference between religion and atheism (I would add, at least not with the atheism which admits the insuperable incomprehensibility of reality). If we take this to be the meaning of the second point, the intellectual difficulties, then the model which underlies this difficulty is in fact the same as the one assumed in the first point about difficulties. In this model, God is simply the second stage of an intellectual process which does not occur until after the apprehension of reality and of the incomprehensibility of its facticity, as a second problem. This means that one can say, without contradicting oneself, that one is simply not going to set out on this march into the second incomprehensibility, on the ground that it has nothing to offer except what one has already learned as an atheist: the incomprehensibility of reality in its inexplicable facticity. But what, as we asked before, if this model is simply wrong? What if the experience of the incomprehensible facticity is already taking place in an anonymous experience of God because this incomprehensibility of the facticity of the world itself can only be experienced in an attempt to go beyond these particular realities, in an intuition which is, unknowingly, already grappling with God? Why is it that we regard the world as something about which we can always ask more questions, something which, in spite of its solid presence, is not obvious at all?

In trying to answer our question, we cannot stop at the world because we have all along already gone beyond the world by treating it, inevitably treating it, as the sum of a set of finite realities distinct from each other. We have asked a question which goes beyond the world, not in the sense that it looks for an answer which would make everything clear and intelligible (such an answer would not be the incomprehensible God of Christianity), but one which leads us into an incomprehensibility which belongs to God. But since it is this incomprehensibility which first makes us aware of the incomprehensibility of the world in its facticity, we cannot say without unwittingly contradicting ourselves, that we will settle for the incomprehensibility of the world and don't need to add to that a second incomprehensibility which we call God. These two incomprehensibilities cannot be identified because the incomprehensibility of the world, like the world itself, is a plural, composite entity, which is completely incapable of making itself intelligible and comprehensible as a single entity through its plurality. To make it intelligible and graspable as a single entity requires a principle which cannot simply be identified with the a posteriori adding up of its individual reality. Whether we can really have dealings with this single original incomprehensibility itself, is of course again another issue, and one which we have already often come up against and will come up against again. Perhaps one could say that anyone who says he or she cannot have any dealings with this incomprehensibility is already having dealings with it by virtue of that statement. But we shall see later that such a relationship with averted face, in which there is perhaps no real difference between religion and a sophisticated atheism, cannot be maintained in human life. The reason is that God has always, in advance, offered the possibility of a positive relation to God—the evidence of this is in the whole history of humanity and of religion.

The third enquiry cites Freud and, with him, sees in the fact that we "have to wish for" God and an eternal life an objection to this conviction of the existence of God. But this is remarkable. If Freud had said that human beings wish that God existed (as Mr X wishes to be Emperor of China), then we might quite justifiably have found such a wish suspicious. But the third enquiry says we have to wish for God and eternal life. Let us accept this "have to" as valid, although the third enquiry in the end makes every effort to tell us that we don't have to have to, but that we can live without illusions even without this wish. But if ultimately we have to wish and in the end even a life which presents itself as a life without illusions is still supported by an undefined hope, which people simply won't admit, then you may ask why is it that this unavoidable wish should be suspicious. On what grounds is it regarded as suspicious, unless one starts from the premise that even the most unavoidable and most obvious things are always suspicious, are essentially a deception and an illusion. Does "the infinitely vast expanse of our longings and wishes" exist or not? And if it exists, which even the third enquiry admits, then this "infinitely vast expanse" in itself says that in advance of the question whether and how it can be filled the condition of its own possibility (even apart from the condition of the possibility of its fulfilment) must exist. We call this condition God.

How is it "more adult" to want to live without the conviction of God's existence? "Adult" is a moral quality, an answer to a moral imperative which claims absolute status. What is the basis for this? Why is such adulthood, on atheist assumptions, more than meaningless stupidity? Why and on what grounds is it implied that the theist is trapped in an illusion, while the sceptical atheist lives without illusions? Is it not more adult to bear to the end, through all disappointments, the conviction of an ultimate meaning which fulfils everything? Can sceptical abstinence from a choice between theism and atheism in the long run take us any further than a life of banality, timidly avoiding the ultimate great questions of existence?

The enquiry goes on to object that the concept of God combines the most mutually contradictory statements and so is empty. First I want to make a comment, which may sound rather abstract, on the more formal side of this objection before we go on to the detailed description which the enquiry gives. If, in Christian belief, God is the incomprehensible mystery and only because he is that is he God, then we may expect in advance that a positive synthesis of the "attributes" predicated of him which makes complete sense to us, not only will not succeed, but also cannot possibly succeed. If we had a clear understanding of the connections between all the things that we say about God as the single source of all the realities and contradictions we experience, then it would be quite certain that our concept was not of God but of something we had constructed to spare us the ultimate act of our existence, which is entrusting ourselves in hope and love to this inexpressible mystery. It is sufficient if we realise that it is not certain that the various statements about God in his infinity and unity as opposed to our own multiplicity are not simply inevitably contradictory, so that if this were so, such a God would quite rightly have to be rejected as a meaningless contradiction. But that the original unity of the multiplicity and its contradictions "beyond" this multiplicity itself is such a contradiction, as opposed to the concept of the mystery, this cannot be proved.

But now to the details of this problem. In the third enquiry in the light of this wretched world of ours and in confrontation with it, the concept of a God who is simultaneously almighty and infinitely good is seen as an absurd contradiction. A God who is omnipotent and yet does not prevent the appalling horrors of our history cannot be an all-compassionate God; an infinitely good God must be envisaged as impotent and so then cannot really be God. There is no doubt that the doubts about God which really touch the core of our existence have their true origin here. There can be no doubt that if one launched, at this point, into a quick and cheap theistic apologetic, one would be rightly asked whether one could bring oneself to utter such words if this appalling torment of creation was tormenting oneself.

And yet is it true that after Auschwitz it is impossible to believe in God? Or is it rather the case that it is precisely after Auschwitz that one must believe in God unless one is going to deny the dead, and all the other victims of a suffering which appears meaningless, their last dignity and significance? If someone denies the existence of God because our world is so appallingly sombre, does this denial make it brighter? Or is this suffocating darkness thereby proclaimed the ultimate and definitive unmeaning of this world, which has no meaning? The atheist, who to support his or her existence keeps on trying to find tiny and pitiful islands of meaning in the sea of black meaninglessness, is forced to attribute to this world more value, splendor, beauty and happiness than the believer in God, who knows in advance that the world which directly confronts him or her certainly does not have to provide from its own resources the final answer to the question of its meaning.

We must honestly admit that the distinction between what God himself brings about and what he merely permits doesn't in the end take us any further here. Under any circumstances, God, as the effective creator, remains responsible for the creaturely freedom which he has created and for the actions of that freedom which he knows "in advance" and must also creatively support. But nevertheless it is not true that the protests of the unhappy against a blissful God who is almighty and good need really be the last word of the creature. Would such a protest have any meaning at all or any legitimacy if it were made in a world of blind and rigid natural laws and accidents in the face of which even to mention a question of meaning would in advance be meaningless?

We are faced with a dilemma. Either we constantly convince ourselves anew that this cry of protest which accompanies the whole history of the world is in fact heard and answered in a way that from our present position we cannot understand, but also cannot disprove, or we can convince ourselves that all these protests are in advance meaningless, that they have no more significance than some physical friction phenomena which come and go. The unhappy man who protests against God ought not to forget that even his protest lives on the implicit hypothesis of God, whom he explicitly denies.

If an unbeliever were to say that he protested only against an almighty and good God, and that without this God the horror that confronts us would on its own be no reason for protest or for real despair, then I would say this unbeliever ought really to try to live out this policy of not complaining in his life and not just in his theory; he would soon find out whether he could really manage it or whether his unhappiness still felt like the sort that covertly called for a God. The "quiet resignation" which the third enquiry praises is also a moral postulate, and I do not see how it could be justified without an explicit or implicit reference to God. Why should I be quietly resigned rather than in a frenzy of protest if in fact in the end both attitudes plunge into the abyss in which nothing can claim any superiority to anything else?

And another point: Do not protests against God and his existence in the name of goodness and love presuppose that we can place God under the law of our own morality and our own claims to life? Don't they presuppose that we regard him as someone who must justify himself to us by our own criteria, whereas if he is really God, he is the very one in whom our concepts, our standards, disappear and these standards and value judgments only retain significance to the extent that we rightly hope that this destruction of our standards in the incomprehensibility of God eventually works for our life and salvation?

And a final remark: We must remember that all the pain and all despair at the darkness of existence, if they overpower a person (which is quite possible) and make a free choice between hope and despair impossible, are in no sense a moral or theological catastrophe or can bring one about. Rather, like infirmity or madness they must be classified with physiological catastrophes which are terrible but do not affect the real existence of a person before God. In other words, in a really Christian interpretation of life they certainly do not consign a person to ultimate futility.

The third enquiry asks me finally about the firmness of my own belief in God. It's not quite clear from this question what precisely is meant by this firmness and unshakeableness but let us do without a more exact definition. My answer would be that in principle and in terms of the doctrine of freedom of belief which is part of the Christian faith, I must naturally expect all my life to be faced with the alternative of either freely believing in God or freely denying his existence. Specifically, as a Christian, if salvation is decided by God himself and not by secondary realities, I may not deny freedom of belief, which is a dogma, with regard to the existence of God. On Christian premises it is wrong to imagine the possibility of a rational demonstration of God's existence as something which drenches me in the radiant light of clarity, overwhelms me and relieves me of the heavy burden of choice.

Naturally Christians must also expect that their choice for or against the existence of God will not be made in the dimension of theoretical reflection and metaphysics, but rather, whatever may be the state of affairs in this dimension, in the unanalysed sphere of practical action in ordinary life. A person who hates his or her neighbour has freely decided against the existence of God in the unanalysed depths of his or her existence, even if the conceptual and verbal system of theism still occupies the front of his or her consciousness and thereby perhaps really serves to prevent the real unbelief from becoming conscious.

But, having said all this and keeping it clearly in mind, I would still say that I see in the realm of my reflective and to some extent prospective consciousness nothing which might be the case or might happen which would make me no longer believe in God. (Naturally I have already dealt with the question of the success of some atheistic "brainwashing". This might perhaps be successful, but this success would have to be relegated to the same impersonal, morally and theologically irrelevant dimension in which we placed the state of being overcome by pain or despair. Naturally, a "brainwashing" of this sort, which is the moral equivalent of inducing an apersonal form of despair of God, may often appear in forms which seem to have nothing at all in common with "brainwashing", for example the pressure of a public opinion which presents itself as obvious. All that these produce is an atheism which is pre-personal and morally irrelevant. But this was only a parenthesis.)

So then, what might shake faith in God? The high points and ecstasies of life proclaim him. The appalling depths no less cry out for him. The banality of everyday life is in the end bearable

copy 1

only in the hope that the life of the spirit, of freedom and love, does not sink finally into this terrible banality. The absolute value of love and loyalty is filled and supported from within by what we call God. All the paths of the future lead to God if they are not to run into nothingness and so make meaningless even the tiny stretches of the way which we manage to cover. It seems to me that God is looking at me and allowing himself to be found in everything. The truth is that a combination of a half yes and a half no gets us nowhere, even though we constantly attempt it because we are weak and weary and also full of the thousand and one half-measures which make up the world and life. The pure Yes which includes everything and excludes from its original unity only nothingness, is called God. We are not him. But it is given to us to believe in him and to risk the leap of trust, hope and love into the depths of his incomprehensibility. Otherwise we would need to have the courage to say the pure No. However, this justifies nothing, and it is hardly possible, or completely impossible, to understand how a human being could find it possible to utter such a pure No. I believe that where the freedom of existence is really found poised in a life, the Yes to God as a pure Yes is easier than the pure No, though our responsibility must always allow for the possibility of the other.

It's terrible. I feel as though I had said as good as nothing about the points raised by the third enquiry. And what I have said was certainly not an initiation into the mystery of how one really encounters God. But, perhaps in either case, a reader will nevertheless have been encouraged to follow a small light in his or her life, the existence of which he can deny only by being dishonest, and to follow it as a promise of the eternal light which we call God and which not only exists but can also be found more and more.

Four

"The invisible gardener"

I f this story didn't already exist it would have had to be invented. Two men on an expedition come into a clearing in the jungle. In this clearing there are many flowers. One of the men claims: "This garden is looked after by a gardener". The other denies this assertion. In order to decide which of the two is right, they pitch their tent in the clearing and keep watch on it day and night. They never see a gardener. Then the first man claims that it must be an invisible gardener. They erect an electrified barbed wire fence around the clearing. But even so, there is no trace of a gardener. Neither do they notice any movement of the fence, such as would indicate an invisible climber, nor do they hear a scream such as would imply that someone had touched the electric fence. Nevertheless the first man sticks to his assertion, which he now modifies in the following way: There is a gardener who is not only invisible, but also inaccessible to all the other senses. At this, the other asks how such a gardener is different from a merely imaginary gardener or no gardener.

God the invisible gardener? When I ask myself why belief in the existence of God is so difficult for us today, one of the main reasons we must mention is the action of God in the world—or rather its absence. How does a "gardener" whose action cannot be perceived differ from a merely imaginary gardener? How does a God who does not intervene in the processes of the world differ from a merely imaginary or a totally non-existent God? Theoretical arguments for or against God have no end. Proposition follows proposition. Objection follows objection.

Both sides can claim a measure of plausibility.

It is different with the action of God. Here, for the men and women of our time, there has been an important and tangible change as a result of the unveiling of nature in the wake of the progress of the exact sciences. Naturally, our ancestors too were aware of laws of nature. And they knew that much can be attributed to human failure. And even if one refuses to attribute to the natural sciences the influence on the religious difficulties of our time which some people ascribe to them, it remains a fact that in spite of everything the people of the past were much more convinced of the possibility of a direct intervention of God in the world than we are. There were too many unusual events, not explicable in this-worldly terms, which could only be made sense of by an intervention of God. To oversimplify, in the past human beings encountered God at every step. They knew where he lived, up above the stars, and they could literally see where his almighty hand worked, namely everywhere that human beings reached the end of their wisdom and knowledge. And that point was quickly reached. A God was needed to keep the stars in the firmament and make it rain at the right time. A God was needed as creator of the human soul and guide of the fate of the world for good or ill. God was the keystone without which the marvellous structure of creation would not hold together.

And then? Then came the rude awakening. The unveiling of nature as a result of the discovery of its regularities soon made it difficult to believe in the gifts and processes of nature as the result of God's actions. The trusting knowledge of being held in God's hand gave way to the realisation that one was at the mercy of a nature without miracles. If I am honest, I have absolutely no expectation that God will intervene for my benefit in the necessary course of the natural laws. When an aeroplane crashes it is not because God wanted it so, but because, for example, it had a crack in the wing. And such knowledge casts its paralysing shadow over any serious petitionary prayer. Even we Christians after all believe that humanity's fight against cancer is not carried on and decided in the monasteries of contemplative orders, but in the laboratories of

universities and hospitals. Why else do Rogationtide processions look so comic to us? Why do votive tablets in shrines
look so old-fashioned?

I'm not at all denying that many people may have the impression that their prayers have been heard by God. Quite the
opposite, I admire such trust. But for myself I cannot honestly
pray that at so many miles an hour my car tires will not burst; I
can't pray that more rice may grow in the paddy fields of Asia,
or that the drought in India may end. And one could go on. I
have no idea—and I say this at the risk of being accused of a
lack of humility and insufficient trust in God—if my prayers
have ever been heard by God. To me he is the invisible gardener whose action in the world, if it takes place at all, is completely undetectable, cannot be perceived in any particular instance. I know of course that there are extraordinary, "para-
psychological" events. That there are more things between
heaven and earth than our petty wisdom dreams of. But what
has that to do with God?

What I am saying is that, more than all the atheistic critique
of religion and its handy arguments, which are worth debating,
the absence of divine activity in the world and in the life of the
individual has led to the uncertainty that we talked about before. Today we are no longer brought up against God. We have
to make a deliberate effort to think about him. God still exists in
the churches, but not where our lives and the most ordinary
events of ordinary life run their course.

Now modern theology—and we may be grateful to it—has
adapted relatively quickly to the changed situation. It distinguishes between a "primary cause" and a "secondary cause". It
says that God cannot act in any other way except through secondary causes—which simply means through the reality of this
world—unless he is to be reduced to the level of his creatures.
This makes some sort of sense to me—but nevertheless I can't
get rid of an uncomfortable feeling: God is now really becoming the invisible gardener in whose action one can believe or
not.

Allow me at least once to quote a passage from your "basic
course in the faith" in which you write about the "accessibility

of God in the world". It is grist to my mill. "I have a good idea", you explain, "which results in an important decision which can be empirically demonstrated and is technically correct. I regard this idea as an illumination from God; have I any right to? I may be led to such a judgment by the suddenness of the idea or by the impossibility of finding a causal or functional explanation for the origin of this good idea. Nevertheless my judgment is ultimately not justified by such a subjective impression. On the contrary, I have the right, yes even the duty, to explain this idea". And you go on to explain that physiological or psychological influences, environmental and other conditions may be a sufficient explanation for the good idea without requiring you to regard it as a particular example of the presence of God in the world. I would accept this completely. But you go further. You do want to see your good idea as the action of God, an "illumination", which is not at all anything extraordinary because God is always active, in the world and in me. The theologians call this action of God a "transcendental action", which in simple terms means precisely an activity remote from human experience, as it were a different dimension, not accessible, which can only be inferred.

It is just this point that all my questions are concerned with, and I want to mention at least a few of them. One objection occurred to me quite spontaneously: If a good idea is to be attributed to God's action, where do the bad ideas come from? Do they also come from God or do they suddenly have no other explanation than human beings? If God is already active always and everywhere, can we simply rule him out when it no longer suits us? And again, and perhaps more importantly, theology likes to operate with propositions which purely because they contain no logical contradiction and can, therefore, be presented as possible, turn possibilities into reality. Of course, all sorts of things might be possible. Why shouldn't there, somewhere in the universe, be little green men with aerials on their heads! Applied to our question, this means: naturally it could be the case. God acts in us and in the world in a way we cannot perceive, guides fates and fortunes, prompts human beings to good and at the same time makes the good possible.

But here too I would like to have, if not proofs, at least credible evidence. Am I wrong when I say that the widespread gap between modern men and women and God (or belief in God) may be attributed to the fact that believers in general are expected to take possibilities as hard cash, while a believer, who has got smart as a result of experience and thinking, no longer accepts this? What specific evidence is there really for any activity by God in the world? Philosophical and theological speculations don't help us here, at least not those people who have neither desire nor energy to embark on philosophical and theological arguments. What I'm saying is that there is quite as much reason to deny the activity of the "invisible gardener" as there is to maintain it. The God of the gaps is dead, the God who was supposed to stop the gaps in our ignorance. And one of Bonhoeffer's frequently quoted remarks seems to me to have consequences which are fatal for any faith which was meant to be lived by. Bonhoeffer said that in the grey light of everyday life human beings had got used to managing without God: they have learnt to cope on their own in all the important matters of life, without invoking the working hypothesis of God.

Let me emphasise this once again, even though it has come up several times already in these discussions. What is the real position? In my first question I said that I don't know what meditation is; Sunday mass bores me; I regard grace before and after meals as a lie; and, even if I can't prove it, many other believers must have similar feelings. Religious practices—to use a general term—are quite often felt as an obligation, not as a need or a burning concern. Don't we envy our unbelieving neighbour who doesn't have to do all that we do, or at least ought to do? But why do we feel like this? Isn't it reasonable to expect some rewards for one's efforts? I would like to feel that my religious practices are not in vain. I would like to know that God—in whatever way—answered, but not in that cheap argument which says that God always answers a prayer, even if the answer doesn't turn out as we would like it, because God always knows better what is for our good. Anyone who argues like that is using an undiluted version of the immunisation strategy. So I carry out my religious exercises—or neglect them—and lose more and more my desire to pray.

But faith is, as has been rightly said, where religion gets serious, because religion doesn't live on theoretical arguments and theological speculations; it lives from a real relation with God. And then everything takes its course. There is no sign of God's activity, and this in turn at least makes it difficult to pray honestly; in any case prayer only takes place in Sunday clothes, not in the ordinary surroundings of factories and offices. And so there begins a loss of contact with God which grows steadily. Alienation. God becomes a stranger. Can we really hold it against the younger generation when they, for the most part, feel able to do without prayer or attending mass? Simply because they can't do anything with any of this, because the God in whom they believe and to whom they are supposed to turn in prayer alters nothing in life. Because he is the "invisible gardener" whose action cannot be perceived and is not obvious. Is there any way out of this almost inevitable sequence of events? Or, in other words, how can the invisible gardener be made visible?

Bertolt Brecht wrote in his *Stories Of Mr. Keuner:* "Someone asked Mr. Keuner whether God existed. Mr. Keuner said: 'I suggest that you consider whether your behaviour would change depending on the answer to this question. If it would not change then we can forget the question. If it would change, then I can help you at least to the point of saying that you have already decided: you need a God' ". You need a God—but only as a result of this belief something in your life changes! What changes as a result of the action of God in the world?

* * *

I readily admit, right from the start and without reservation, that the fourth enquiry deals with a completely fundamental topic within the issue of the existence of God. I admit this willingly even though the story of the invisible gardener doesn't shock me as much as this enquiry perhaps imagines. For the allegory to make a greater impression, we would need to know what reasons the first man had for assuming that this clearing in the jungle had been artificially laid out.

It must be admitted, and again right at the start, that with regard to the relation of God to the world a fundamental change has taken place or is still taking place, not only in non-Christian ideas, but also within Christianity and its theology. We, yes we Christians too, are slowly getting used to not finding interventions of God within our world which can be pinpointed in space and time. Even for Christians today, God is not a particular element within reality as a whole which has an "effect" of such a sort that this effect and its direct origin in God can be observed. Instead, God is a pre-condition which supports the multiplicity of the world, including the mutual influence on each other of the particular realities of the world, without belonging to this system as an individual element. If this is so, and if people used to believe that God, at least in particular cases, intervened at particular points in the course of the world in a way which could be located in space and time, then there has really been an enormous change in outlook between previous times and our own, and the effects of this change have not yet been completely felt either in ordinary religious practice or in Christian theology, and that is why they are still causing us considerable difficulties today.

Nevertheless, even this change in mentality should not be exaggerated. Even traditional theism taught the immediate presence of God in all things, the immediate maintenance of all things by an ever-present creative act of God, the immediate cooperation of God with all the activity of finite realities. This image of God was very far from an idea of God which regards him as being outside the world (after it has been created) and only now and again intervening in its mechanism with identifiable acts of power and miracles, or by setting the course of nature and history in such a way that we can never attribute either to an "accident" or specifiable causes within the world. Even the old traditional image of God presented a God who was not a particular, however powerful, individual cause within the totality of reality, but an all-embracing ultimate ground which, by definition, could not be confused with the total of particular realities or included in it. However, wrong though it may be to exaggerate the difference between the traditional and the modern image of God, it is nevertheless true that the old image of God did also envisage as a matter of course interventions of God which could be located at points in space and time, and also believed itself able to detect such interventions immediately and certainly, at least in the case of "miracles". Today, however, not just the human sciences, but ordinary human common sense, postulate that where a particular new phenomenon appears in the world of human experience it can and must be derived from another phenomenon which belongs to the world and which will be the cause of the first, and not attributed to a particular intervention of God. The only possible question this leaves is whether this-worldly cause can already be described more exactly and made accessible to empirical experience, or must provisionally be postulated as not yet known but in principle knowable.

If we ignore for the moment some reservations which we shall want to make later, we can accept this modern mentality as given. It naturally gives rise to undeniably major difficulties for the traditional outlook. Is not the miracle faith's favourite child? But can faith in the traditional Christian sense continue if we do without miracles at least in the traditional sense? Can we seriously still think of salvation history as the action of God on the world and history with their reactions to that action? An action not of the world, but on the world? Is petitionary prayer, which plays such an important part in Christianity from the Our Father on, still conceivable when this petitionary prayer seems to postulate an intervention of God which would not take place without it? Has God any real meaning for us if we are to forget about these constantly new and unexpected, particular interventions locatable at particular points in space and time, and envisage him only as the ultimate cause of everything, always hidden behind the world, silent and incomprehensible? Does not this make the problem we have now so often come up against so great as to be insurmountable? Does not God now become so unfathomably and incomprehensibly distant from us that a modest atheism which accepts all the uncertainties and a theism aware of its difficulties cannot really be distinguished? Is it possible to embark on a relationship with a God who no longer shows any signs of himself as a particular element in the world? This is, after all, what all religions practice. I do see the problem though I perhaps express it with less emotion than can be seen in the fourth enquiry.

Can Christianity, can any religion at all, continue, if God does not appear in our realm of experience as one among all the other realities with effects and manifestations which belong, and can belong, only to him? First, before we consider how Christianity and religion are conceivable or practicable under these new assumptions, I would like to make one reservation. If God is God, the mystery which by definition we cannot compass, whom we naturally cannot comprehend even though we constantly stray into his incomprehensibility, can we really tell him that he is unable or not allowed to show himself in this world as an individual because this contradicts our "concept" of him? Naturally we can say that as long as God does not show himself to us in his own incomprehensible and infinite reality, he must give us signs of his existence through a particular finite reality. However, such a reality, because it is finite, can necessarily be imagined as in principle caused by another finite reality, and so it tells nothing at all about God in addition to the totality of the world, even when we assume, that worldly reality as a whole carries in itself a reference to God. But are we sure that this argument is conclusive if all along we realise that God is the incomprehensible? Let us leave this reservation on one side and consider only on our initial assumption whether Christianity is conceivable and practicable if God is envisaged only as the pre-condition of the world as a whole and not as a particular reality present within the world. Having defined and circumscribed the question in this way, let us first consider it quite generally, i.e., we shall not for the moment ask whether in such a view salvation history and "miracles" are still conceivable (and if so how).

First we must remind ourselves again that the demonstration of the existence of God which was previously offered at least in outline does not lead to a God who fits into the totality of all reality as a particular reality and is in mutual interaction with these other realities. We did point out, though very briefly, that we cannot infer the existence of God by invoking a general principle of a sufficient cause, as used elsewhere in our knowledge, as the mere end point of a causal chain as we normally imagine one. No, God is necessarily affirmed, though in an unanalysed and inexplicit way, as the condition of the possibility of any knowledge or freedom. Knowledge and freedom are possible, even in an individual act, because they reach out without limit to the one infinity of being which we call God. If these ideas are right, then we are always dealing with a God who does not appear here and there in his world, but always has already appeared always and everywhere. When we come into contact with a reality, it is, even if generally inexplicitly, contrasted with its infinite presupposition, with God, who is the silent strangeness which surrounds, permeates and supports everything. The silent gardener who tends the clearing of the world has no need to climb over the fence surrounding the clearing; the clearing just cannot be imagined without him. He is not in it here or there, rather he is so anonymously there that he really cannot be looked for in a particular place, and it requires a supreme, though genuine and necessary, effort to distinguish him once again from what, if it is really imagined and understood, cannot possibly be conceived without him.

And so we are back, it seems to me, with the old problem that has been worrying us for so long. How can we have any contact with this God? How, when, as all Christians say and in their lives always forget, it is he who is responsible for the ideas and the attitudes with which I appeal to him? If I imagine him as he must be imagined, as the free creative ultimate ground of myself, must I not imagine myself as his puppet, totally in his power, incapable of having a relationship with the person that pulls the strings, because any such relationship would once again be his work and not mine? Should I appeal for an explanation to the hard fact of religion? Is the distinctive feature of God's creative work, which is also part of his incomprehensibility, and what distinguishes it from our own creativity, that "He" can create what is really different from himself, autonomous, and that it is only when we try to imagine this that we can really imagine the uniqueness of divine causality? Can one really keep this in mind in one's religious life without imaging the true God as too small and ourselves as too big or making the opposite mistake? Can we talk to God without being struck dumb by the appalling thought that it is really he who is speaking, he for whom the world is really only a game that he is running as his own and not as ours? And if all these ideas leave us confused, is it then not the best thing, and the most appropriate to God, not to deny God (which would be stupid), but, with our faces humbly averted from God, patiently to remain within the narrow confines of our existence, to be, on theistic grounds, humble atheists?

But by talking in this way we have already gone over the limits which we claim we want to keep, we have already begun to have contact with God in spite of saying that it's better to remain at a distance from him and leave him alone in his own glory and bliss. There is no God who tramples around as a lonely figure in the clearing of our existence and who can be discovered by the electrified wires of our specialised sciences. Nevertheless God exists, and we are in touch with him when we say this and even when we assert that the whole idea of being in contact with him is impossible.

We have to make the great leap forward. We must simply get involved with him, launch ourselves at him, pray to him: then, but only then, will we realise that what is conceptually impossible is possible because it is. Of course Christians know and say that all this is ultimately possible because in real reality God and human beings are not related simply as two contrasting realities which have to meet only after existing separately. Nor do Christians say simply that God is always already in touch with these contrasting realities because he creates, maintains, and supports them by his creative power. Christians believe that the real movement of the creature towards God is not just brought about by God as something separate from God, but is also supported all along by God's own reality. (Therefore, for the religious person, as opposed to the speculative metaphysician, it in the end does not matter how we answer the question whether and how this real encounter between God and a human being can be envisaged, even in an inadequate way, unless God himself, by his own reality—called grace—is supporting this movement of the creature towards God. This is what guarantees that this movement will really reach God himself.) This support, by the reality of God himself, for whatever action the creature takes in the direction of God is what, in current theological jargon, is called grace. Naturally there is no time to discuss it in more detail at this point. It is mentioned here only to make clear that Christian theology has not forgotten how difficult it is to maintain the idea that the movement of the spirit really goes in the direction of God himself and not merely towards a conceptual and verbal idol of God, of which we have no idea what its point is or whether it might not be better to relieve ourselves of all this strain on the mind and heart.

From this crucial appeal to activity in which we simply do have contact with God, let us turn back for a moment to theory. It is said to be impossible to discover God in the world; that is the difficulty. We replied that the reason he cannot be discovered as a particular phenomenon is that he is the prior condition of possibility of any sort of knowledge, in other words that, because he is as such the condition of searching, he does not need to be looked for as though he had not yet in any sense been found. He is not a bit of our empirical world, but the subjective and objective, always prior, condition for the existence of an empirical world. Paradoxical as it may sound, he cannot be found because he already has been found always and everywhere, whether or not a person is able to realise this explicitly and express it in words and particular concepts. If we look at the matter in this way, the question whether it is easy to detect the gardener in the clearing of our existence, or whether complicated methods are required, is inherently meaningless. The real question is whether a person is willing to face the conceptual and emotional effort of being sensitive to the movement into the illimitable incomprehensibility of God which is inevitably present in all human activity, or impatiently rejects it as too much effort. In the latter case the only question is whether this indifference can really be maintained through-

out life or not. In any case people must consider that the refusal to be concerned with the problem of God is in itself an
attitude to it, and it is only possible for people to be carefree
atheists if they have simply never heard of theism and atheism.
And the real question is, secondly, whether it is possible to have
contact with this God who is always and everywhere silently
present.

The fourth enquiry accuses normal Christian petitionary
prayer of hypocrisy, evidently on the ground that a modern
person cannot seriously imagine changing God's mind (if he
exists), getting him to revise his plans, so that (as someone once
suggested) the weather would be different in Tibet if pious
South Tyroleans with their processions were transplanted
there. But do Christians think of their petitionary prayer in this
way, and must they think of it in this way? To give an honest
answer to this question we must certainly admit that in religion
as it is practised there is usually element of magic, conjuring,
the frantic effort of the poor creature to avert something which
it doesn't want to happen at any price by invoking God. It
would be wrong to deny these ingredients in religion as it
exists, though in among them genuine religion may nevertheless be being practised, even if it is not "chemically pure". This
sort of religion is still a thousand times better than the triviality
of the average man or woman who anxiously tries to avoid all
experiences which come from the unfathomable depths of his
or her existence—and these are religious experiences.

But what happens in true petitionary prayer when it is part
of genuine religion? Human beings face the incomprehensible
plan of their existence, which they accept as at once incomprehensible and yet as originating in the wisdom and love of
God; however it may turn out, whether it brings life or death,
people then have a sense of themselves, with their own identity
and vital impulses, as willed by God, without wanting to produce or force an intelligible synthesis between their vital impulses and the plan of their existence. And so they say Yes to
the incomprehensibility of God and to their own will to live,
without wanting to know how the two fit together. The unity of
the two, which is not something that we can create, is petition-

ary prayer, since it is only prayer if it says radically, "Your will, not mine", and it would not be petitionary prayer if it did not dare to ask God for something which we had thought of ourselves. Petitionary prayer is thus simply actualising the incomprehensibility of human existence which, down to the last fibre, comes from God alone and goes out to him, yet is such that it can hold its own before God and not be destroyed.

Why should we be suspicious of petitionary prayer if it is in fact simply the actualisation of the incomprehensibility of the creature before God? It is not an attempt to change God's mind and yet it has a meaning. And this meaning does not need to be saved by the explanation that God has foreseen petitionary prayer and included it in his plans for the world and so already made a causal connection between the answer and the prayer. Nor does the meaning of petitionary prayer need to be made plausible by an appeal to an atomistic indeterminism and chance which give God freedom of movement without infringing on the laws of nature. With or without such accidents or indeterminism, the world as a whole and in all its particulars is the expression of the incomprehensible control of God and as such is accepted in petitionary prayer as meaningful.

We have not yet said anything about the possibility for existence of the events people call miracles, although this is a subject which could certainly be discussed in connection with the fourth enquiry. However, since miracles (whatever the precise meaning of this word may be) are usually treated within Christianity as a legitimation of the history of salvation and revelation as such (at least in modern Catholic fundamental theology), the subject of miracles can quite well be postponed to a later point in our discussion. This naturally applies all the more to the question of how salvation history and the history of revelation can be reconciled with the assumption that God does not intervene in the otherwise secular course of the world at particular, specially marked points of time and space.

Finally, I'm going to read through your fourth enquiry again and make a few remarks on odd sentences here and there. You say, "I have absolutely no expectation anymore that God will intervene for my benefit in the necessary course of the natural law". I don't expect this either, but I do expect an actual course of the world, which because it is actual does not have to be shown to be necessary, which is favourable to my free development towards my final identity before God, and will in fact be so if I accept it as meaningful in a final choice of meaning through a trusting acceptance of God's incomprehensibility. Is that meaningless? Is such a life not different, though perhaps not in the trivial details of everyday life, from what it would be if left in the conviction that it was only a—completely inexplicable—flash of ultimate meaninglessness, before this flash too disappeared in an empty night? If we seriously compare these two lives, and also unfold the life of the Godless person to its ultimate consequences, so that it is not just a momentary petulant theory on the surface of a life which is fed essentially by quite other sources, is it then true that God exists only in the Churches, but not in the everyday round of our lives? When one looks at the honest and courageous lives that most people lead, which mere atheism could not possibly justify, must one not say that their fulfilment comes from a belief in the "unknown God" whose image stands on the altars of the hearts even of those who think they have to be atheists?

When modern theology (and mediaeval theology too) distinguishes between "primary cause" and "secondary causes", it is not trying to create a refuge for a God who can no longer be discovered as a particular cause within the world. What it is doing is taking to a final conclusion the old realisation, without which no genuine concept of God can be imagined, namely the knowledge that God is not a bit of the world, but the one and only ground of all particular realities, who permeates everything and supports everything. What objection could there be to my applying this realisation to a good idea which is important to my life, which originates in God precisely because it is linked with all other worldly reality in this-worldly causality?

You object that then a bad idea also has to be attributed to the action of God. This objection is directed to a problem which has been discussed in Christianity for almost 2000 years and certainly has not found a solution in the sense that, after hearing the answers offered someone might say, "Yes it's all clear now". I could give you the traditional teaching. According to this, in so far as any reality (in the moral order too) is real, it derives from a creative action of God. On the other hand, in so far as an evil action contains, in addition to its positive elements, something non-existent, negative, something that ought not to exist, and only so is evil because the formal badness of an action as such is something negative, it requires no creative collaboration from God.

This answer of the Christian tradition is not wrong and not stupid. Nevertheless we are not obliged for that reason to claim that it solves the problem of heart and mind in the face of moral evil in the world. One might even fear that such an answer, if it were taken seriously and on its own, was really speculating the immense seriousness of moral evil out of the world. The only other remark to be made is that the simultaneous total dependence of the world in being and existence on God and its true autonomy as other than God is a basic fact. It cannot be understood from some superior position and the radical dependence even of evil on God and his originality is in fact its climax. But is the "mystery of evil" a reason to doubt the origin of all reality in God?

I want to protest against your implication that theology acts arbitrarily and, without any proof or demonstration, turns logical possibilities into realities by sleight of hand. It's remarkable that you ask for specific evidence of the action of God in the world and assert, at the same time, that philosophical and theological speculations are no use to you, particularly since there are many people who have neither desire nor time to engage in philosophical and theological reflection. Is a piece of reasoning false or idle simply because there are people who say they have neither the time nor energy to engage in it? Have you the right to dismiss an argument offered in advance as "speculation" simply because Philistines feel it's too much for them? The demonstration of the existence of God and the demonstration of his action in the world and the difference between this and particular causal or functional connections within the world are naturally identical. The assertion of the existence of a single underlying ground of all realities and of an understanding of them, an underlying ground which, as the condition of the possibility both of the world and of the understanding of the world, is always implicitly presupposed in every particular act of knowledge, is naturally also in itself the assumption of an all-pervading and all-supporting action of God, who is the force of the world without thereby being an individual cause in it.

You appeal to Bonhoeffer. The quotation you give needs to be handled carefully and we need to look closely to see what it really means and what it doesn't mean. When Bonhoeffer knelt in prayer as he waited for his executioner, that was certainly not an atavistic relapse from his theology. He knew no God of the gaps, either for the course of the world or for his knowledge. But it is where this God of the gaps disappears that the true God emerges. Why should it be a perfect example of the "immunisation strategy" when a theologian says that God always answers a really genuine prayer, even if possibly in a way different from what the petitioner had imagined? If the answer to any prayer were an empirically determinable datum to be measured by the intentions of the prayer, if this sort of appeal to God, looking for this sort of answer, could still be called prayer, then certainly immunisation strategy to justify prayer would be the right description. But suppose that prayer, in spite of the creature's cry for help which it contains, is in advance an absolute surrender to the incomprehensible God, to his incomprehensible, if good, dispositions and only so can be called prayer. Suppose that prayer of this sort is regarded as meaningful as a test case of faith. In these circumstances the remark that God answers prayer in accordance with his incomprehensible wisdom and love is not an a posteriori move in an apologia for petitionary prayer, but in fact the primary and most important statement about its true nature. It has nothing at all to do with an immunisation strategy.

Of course, one must be able to realise that the unconditional surrender of a human being to the incomprehensible will of God who saves and liberates, in other words prayer as the test case of faith in the true God, is meaningful, indeed is the only thing which reconciles the ultimate meaningfulness of existence and its incomprehensibility. If we look at prayer, and in particular petitionary prayer, in this way, then the only question is where and when it can be given a real place in the ordinary dreary lives of men and women. It is perfectly possible in principle to be a Christian and a person who prays even if one has no desire to pray before every snack.

Let God answer, you demand. For there to be an answer, must he answer in such a way that the answer is a particular individual event in my sphere of experience (which I would then of course speedily fit back into the uninterrupted chain of this-worldly connections)? But suppose I attempt to make contact with God; that is when I silently transcend, freely and relaxed, all individual realities, acknowledging their importance but yet aware of their relativity. Suppose that, by such an act of transcendence, I reach the silent incomprehensibility of the most simple fulness and obviousness. If this transcendence by sovereign freedom is not theoretical speculation in words about something, but an act of life, performing this sovereign act of transcendence in its deadly radicalness and not just talking about it, if this ultimate act is experienced as supported and given power by the very mysterious infinite reality into which it lets itself sink, if (moreover) we know that in Jesus Christ, who was crucified and rose again, we have a guarantee that this act will reach this silent incomprehensibility, is not God then experienced? Must I then, in the domain of my everyday experience, look for another invisible gardener who plants this or that separately in the clearing which makes up the area of my own ordinary life? Wouldn't such a God in the end be precisely the one that we are not looking for because the true God must be the one who is all in all in original unity, who supports and empowers everything and not just this or that?

As we have already remarked, this still does not make it clear how this true and real God, who is not obliged to announce himself through our alarm systems, can still be a God of salvation history. This must be discussed later. And when, further, we allow God to be the God who is not subordinate to our creaturely systems and their distinctions, then, it seems to me, we may in the end leave open the question of whether we have to make a critical distinction between the one true God, whom we always mean, who exists always and everywhere, and the God of history and miracles, or whether in fact it should be completely the other way. But at any rate, if and insofar as my life is open, unconditionally and in confidence, to God's incomprehensibility, my life has certainly fundamentally changed in comparison with the life of someone who, in ultimate fear or in appalling triviality, only ever knows this and that particular to which he or she must cling desperately.

Five

Preliminary questions about Christian belief in revelation

O ur discussion—my questions and your answers—must now turn to the central point of the Christian faith, that event in world history from which our faith gets its name and its content: Jesus of Nazareth. I must admit straight away, I cannot engage in polemics against the person of Jesus, nor do I want to. Not through any fear of seeming blasphemous, but simply because this person compels too much attention and respect, because I neither can nor wish to doubt the honourable nature and honesty of Jesus' character and aims. And I know that this polite reticence about the person of Jesus is something that brings me close to the ideas of many people today, but not to the teaching of the Christian Churches.

Jesus of Nazareth? Much greater claims are made for him. He was not one prophet among many, not just a religious genius, not even a mere advocate of renewal, a reformer of a legalistic Jewish religion which was suffocating in formalism. Nor was he just a person who preached attractive and desirable ideals of human life. No, he was God himself, the son of God, God and man in one. Nor do I want at this point to get involved in speculations about how something like this can be imagined, how somebody can be at the same time God and a human being, or how the one God can exist in several persons. If this fact exists, then—it seems to me—it is bound to lie beyond our imaginative capacity, perhaps even beyond the range of our logic, so that contradictions which we think are inevitable are no longer contradictions.

I want to begin this enquiry from a point which may recall several things which have already come up in the previous chapters. I often ask myself, quite honestly, why do we have to have all this performance? Of course, I am not God, and we can always say that he must know what he's doing and why he's doing it, and good for the person that can accept it. But you know the saying—it's meant to be a joke but still brings out real experience and problems—which says God may have made the world—but that's no reason for him to give himself ideas. What's it supposed to mean? Simply that the world is just not such that from it and from our lives we can infer the omnipotence and total goodness of a God who is a Father. To put it crudely once again, if I were God, I would have done it better, made a better job of it! I wouldn't have created a world which—isn't that Christian teaching?—isn't the best possible. Or the other way around, I would have made the best of all possible worlds.

But what would the best sort of world look like? I couldn't say exactly. All the same, whenever I get involved in discussions about suffering and misery in the world and in individual lives (and that's quite often), whenever I ask myself why things in the world are not better, I choose the quickest way. And this way is the question, why did God not create human beings and put them straight into heaven? It all comes down to this. If the vision of God, being with God forever, is in itself the goal of a human life, then why this wearisome—no the word is too weak—this awful and crucial detour through an earthly life? Great writers can put the point better; in Dostoyevsky's *Brothers Karamazov* there is the following passage: "Too high a price has been placed on harmony. We cannot afford to pay so much for admission. And therefore I hasten to return my ticket of admission. . . . It is not God that I do not accept, Alyosha. I merely most respectfully return him the ticket". So why is this ticket stamped "freedom"? Couldn't God have done without "tickets", tickets for eternal life, when no one in the end knows whether they are valid or not? It's funny. If you follow this line further, then it seems that the luckiest people must be those who died as baptised infants, and everyone else may regret that they ever reached the age of reason, of personal responsibility and real freedom.

But now to the next question. Let us suppose that being created to be put directly into heaven isn't a possibility—for whatever reason—this brings me to the point I want to make, about God's saving action in the world. In front of me I've got the little book of meditations by your pupil and friend Karl Lehmann, *Jesus Christ Is Risen* (by the way, it's very good). The book talks about suffering in the world, and one section is headed, "The Only Answer: Consider Jesus". All right. A Christian knows this, even when he can't put it as well as a theologian. But isn't this again still dodging the question which ought to come before "considering Jesus"? We take things as they are and make the best of them. And—let us hope—we're also grateful for God's call to salvation and God's saving action in the world. The call to what we, for want of better words, call "supernatural life", is and remains the free gracious decision of God. But I still ask myself—and the question becomes more difficult when we consider Jesus: Why does God have to intervene in history in a particular way which makes historical events the "loci" of his (supernatural) revelation? And, how credible are the sources of revelation really?

As far as the first part of the question is concerned, we need do no more than start from the general belief of the Church that God desires the salvation of all human beings. If this is true and we take the statement seriously, then from then on this saving will of God's is not—as it may be with human beings—a declaration of good will which stays in God's heart, but necessarily a reality in human beings, all human beings. What God wills is automatically reality. So why a particular salvation history? Could not God bring about the salvation of all men simply through an act of will? Could he not just as well have "decreed" what he brought about through the bringers of revelation and above all through Jesus? Isn't God here again choosing an unnecessarily roundabout way?

I don't think this question is as simple as it may sound at first. In the first place it contains the problem of the knowability of a revelation of God (more about this in a minute!) and, secondly, its implications connect with an attitude which is very widespread today. This could be summed up as follows: there are always people who feel a special call and who do succeed to stir their contemporaries, in all periods, in every religion or world-view. But, in the Judaeo-Christian view, these "prophets" are not recognised as true bringers of revelation. They are not included among those who speak in the name of God and on his behalf. Something in me (and, I think, in many people) rebels against this disparagement of these people and the religions based on them and their teaching. Who today can, and who would want to, denounce the non-Christian religions as the work of the devil? But this was the teaching of the Catholic Church until very recently. So, the implication is: Why does God have to appoint particular bringers of revelation in addition to what is achieved by his will to save? Of course people usually say we need the true religion, to know God's true intentions. But we could equally well ask why that's so important. Might not God be satisfied if people look for him honestly and sincerely? Why must there be one true religion? Why only one way and not many?

All these points are brought to a head by the second question, which we hinted at earlier. How do we recognise a revelation as the revelation of God? I have no objection to the fact that the Jewish religion claims to be the revealed religion. But, while I'm not a specialist on the Old Testament or ancient Eastern religions, I would still say I just haven't got reliable evidence. After all, we know what period the Jewish belief in revelation grew up in. We know how ready people were three thousand years ago to see the action of God, how imagination took over where knowledge was still inadequate. If we cut out of the Jewish religion all the mythological elements and all the fantastic "miracles", I wonder what is left of the proof of a divine revelation to Israel. I wonder what difference there is between a prophet and the particularly religious people of other religions who have existed in the past and still exist (probably down to today). And something else. I sometimes ask myself how I can recognise an (alleged) revelation as a revelation of God. It's not good enough for me—and who would hold it against me?—that a person should be convinced that he is speaking in the name of God; that person can be mistaken about this sort of thing, without setting out to deceive. I am always surprised that it's all so terribly human. So human that it could be interpreted in other ways as well. If God reveals himself, as he must do if he doesn't put us human beings straight into heaven and also doesn't give each person as much revelation as he or she needs to find the way to God on his or her own, why does the God who reveals himself not appear in history in a totally different way? Why not in power and glory or, if that sounds too rhetorical, at least a bit more accessibly?

Behind this question is the matter of faith in Jesus Christ, but it is about the possibility, the necessity and the knowability of a revelation of God. When we confess as Christians that the final and unsurpassable word of God's revelation has been spoken to us human beings in Jesus, we are admitting precisely this: the necessity, the possibility, the knowability of revelation. But I ask if it is really necessary. Couldn't it have been done in a different way? And, cannot God, if he reveals himself in history (apart from what anyone can know about God), himself be known more clearly, "more accessibly"?

That will probably do us, but let me once again quote P. L. Berger. He touches on at least the second part of this question when he writes: "The redeeming presence of God in the world is manifested in history, but it is not given once and for all in the particular historical events reported on in the New Testament. I am . . . constrained to disregard the insistence of the New Testament authors that redemption lies only 'in this name' of Jesus Christ (that is, the name that links the historical figure with the cosmic scope of God's redeeming presence". Or, in my own words, I cannot see—and this is still a preliminary to the question of faith in Jesus Christ—why God chose these roundabout ways, roundabout and difficult ways, to salvation. I may not have succeeded in putting this as clearly as I had hoped, but I think the problems are clear.

* * *

The fifth enquiry—rightly—starts right from the beginning with the fundamental issue of Christianity, faith in Jesus Christ. But then the enquiry concerns itself mainly with problems connected with the possibility and meaning of a history of revelation and salvation in general. Again this is right, because one ought to have considered these more general questions if one wants to discuss problems of Christology, and in this way one's thought also follows the course of the history of revelation. This perhaps justifies limiting the answer to the fifth enquiry to these more general questions about the history of revelation and the history of salvation.

First, however, another remark about the protest against the world as the creation of a wise and benevolent God which we recorded at the beginning in Dostoyevsky's words. God has not, it must be admitted, created the best of all conceivable worlds. But what real purpose would it have if we tried to maintain an ultimate and definitive protest against this world and its creator because we want a better world, a world without suffering? Is this protest inherently so rational and legitimate that it follows from it that no creator God can exist or that he is not wise and benevolent? Is the world brighter, more intelligible and more acceptable if this protest leaves it shut in on itself, in its pain and its disappointment? What justification and what meaning could we claim for such a protest if, when God does not exist, there is no justification or clear criterion for a criticism of this world? Is it not in the end naïve and primitive to envisage a perfection or perfectibility of human beings without freedom? Does it make any sense to imagine perfection and definitive identity in any other terms than as the result of freedom? (For my part I'd rather put a question mark of ignorance beside the fate of children who die before the age of reason, if there are any, than conclude from their existence that there could be a beatific perfection even without freedom, and that God would have done well to bestow this perfection on human beings in this way.) If, through the creative power of God, who provides the motive force for the world from its deepest core, this world is continually coming to its true identity as a whole in an enormous process, then the state towards which it is advancing is freedom, and in that case the world's coming to its true identity in spirit and freedom in spiritual subjects is not just an arbitrary bit of the world which could be removed from it without leaving it meaningless.

Even if someone regards these speculations as too much effort, though in themselves they make very good sense, the fact remains that we confront this world as it is, that in understanding it as it is we necessarily enter into the incomprehensibility of God and his freedom. It therefore makes no sense for us to try to insert this God once more as a totally intelligible element in our calculation which we can then use to demonstrate that the world ought to be different from the way we find it in fact. What we really can and must do is answer the question whether we can find the courage and the energy, in and despite this world, to launch out without reservation into incomprehensibility and treat it as something which would support us and bring us happiness. At any rate, it seems to me, we can see that the free acceptance of this God in the incomprehensibility of his nature and his will is not a ticket for eternal life, a ticket which God could also generously have given us free, but the actual entry into eternal life. I say this even though I am totally at a loss to say what happens to children who die before the age of reason. In this case at least I can always ask whether Christian teaching definitely obliges me to believe in the "immortality" of these "souls", or whether it is certain that God's gracious gift of their happiness in this case is not the grace of free acceptance of the incomprehensibility of God as our happiness.

But now let us get down to some considerations on the history of salvation and revelation in general which the fifth enquiry suggests to us.

It is true, and has to be admitted by any unprejudiced observer, that the traditional idea of the history of salvation and

revelation was in the past based mainly on the model of interventions by God at specific points in space and time in an
otherwise secular history. The world is below and, in spite of its
being created by God, is set on the course of its secularity,
freedom and sin. God is above. He sees this most unsatisfactory
course of history in secularity, error and sin, and decides, since
this course which the world is taking is highly dangerous and
leading to ultimate disaster, to intervene in it at particular
points. The prophets, in his name and by means of a unique
relationship with him, proclaim the truth of salvation which
human beings have corrupted or which they are totally incapable of attaining. He also uses institutions of salvation firmly
inserted spatially and temporally in general history, such as the
covenant with the chosen people of Israel, and miracles which
confirm these prophets and these special institutions of salvation as really deriving from God. It follows that part of this
model of salvation and salvation history was the gratuitous
selection of individuals from the great mass of sinners who
were left behind, even if abandoning them in their sinfulness
was a just judgment.

Now it cannot be said that the traditional image of the history
of salvation and revelation was determined exclusively and, so
to say, in chemical purity by these basic models, that in the
tradition as it existed in the past there were no other elements
which provide a basis for criticising and going beyond these
basic models. Nor can it be maintained that these basic models
were not and are not useful for exploring fundamental Christian truths which cannot be abandoned. The image of the history of revelation and salvation, in which God was the gardener
who appeared at particular points in space and time in the
secular clearing of world history, also knew that God desires
the salvation of all human beings and certainly makes it possible, in all periods and at all places in history, for him to pour
out his spirit on all flesh always and everywhere. It knew that
because salvation must be and is possible everywhere, faith,
hope and love as immediate contact with God, who communi-
cates himself as the content and goal of the spiritual creation,
must be possible always and everywhere. It knew that the his-

tory of the human race, despite "original sin", is not just the history of a race sunk without grace in secularity and its own guilt, but always and everywhere history under the action of the God who takes the form of the deepest energy of the world. There was always a universalistic and a particularistic basic model of the history of salvation and revelation, and the two were never completely and consciously reconciled. On the other hand, it would be wrong to say that the conceptual model of an intervention of God which took place only at this point, and then gradually spread from this one point in the world into all history, was simply *the* basic model by which the history of salvation was to be imagined, or the only model. Equally, this is not to deny that the particularistic basic model was the dominant one, and remains so today. But is this basic model in itself absolutely obligatory? Must it be retained forever? Again, this is not a plea for this model to be simply abandoned.

There is a genuine history of salvation in which not all events are equally important. This history has a direction, breaks, enters into an irreversible stage. All this can and must be said even if we do not imagine this history as a chain of intermittent interventions of God, but as the history of the God who has inserted himself all along into the very core of the world he has created, and has from there been propelling the history of this world towards its perfection. The idea of election retains its legitimacy even if salvation history is not treated as the rescue by an external force of a few individuals from a *massa damnata* hopelessly sunk in sin. Grace as God's loving self-communication remains free election, an unquestionable gift. It makes no difference whether it is given to many or to few, whether from the core of the world it liberates the human race's history of freedom and opens it toward God himself or acts on this history of freedom from the outside. There may, therefore, be no need to abolish this traditional particularistic double model of revelation and salvation, but it can nevertheless be said that in our period it is slowly but surely losing its predominance in favour of a universalistic basic model in which God in his free grace, from the very beginning and always and everywhere, has communicated himself to his creation as its innermost energy and works in the world from inside out.

As evidence of this change of attitude and its legitimacy we may cite not only the religious outlook of Christianity today, but also, for example, important statements of the Second Vatican Council. One may entertain certain reservations about the attitude of Christianity as it actually exists throughout the world, one may hear too little today in the average sermon about the possibility of eternal damnation, of guilt before God, which neither sociology nor psychology can dissolve, of God's judgment. Nevertheless, it is legitimate for this preaching to present the course of world history first as the history of God's love advancing victoriously towards its goal, a history in which God gives himself, and not as a sort of victory won only with great effort by God over his opponent, the evil one. It is totally legitimate for the idea of a merely sporadic intervention of God, which was inevitably seen both spatially and temporally as restricted to quite small areas of the world and its history, to arouse the suspicion of being incredible mythology and an overly anthropomorphic idea of God. One can't very well feel oneself to be chosen by the love of God if one can't also see reasonably clearly a possibility of salvation for everyone else.

One may ask how a history of God's salvation existed in what must have been millions of years between "Adam" and Moses, since even then a history of revelation and a history of religion must have been necessary conditions for salvation. However, even Vatican II made an elegant silent leap from Adam to Moses, that is, it leapt over by far the longest period of human history, with a vague reference to God's providence. A man or woman of today will probably have no trouble in accepting the Old Testament version of the history of Israel as a history of God's dealings with this nation. They will, however, find it hard to regard this covenant as simply and solely and without any qualification the exclusive privilege of that nation, with the histories of all other peoples relegated to a profane sphere. Men and women today therefore do not try to teach God how to use the freedom with which he orders world history (particularly since human history, which brings quite enough differences into history, is also, as a whole and in all its manifestations, the free choice of God). Nevertheless, where history as such is concerned they do have the impression that, failing a rigorous proof of the opposite, the historical differences as such should be attributed in the first place to human freedom. Since the history of salvation and of revelation must be universal (because salvation takes place everywhere, and salvation without faith, that is, without revelation in the strict sense, is impossible), why should there not be events in that history completely analogous to the old covenant of the Israelites? Why should there not be elsewhere in the history of the human race religions, bearers of religious impulses and writings which, for their particular historical situation, had the same sort of legitimacy which we recognise in the old covenant of Israel with its prophets, religious institutions and sacred writings? If it is obvious that not all the elements in any history are equally important or of positive religious value, there is nothing to stop us from recognising in history phenomena of differing importance and differing, indeed even opposite, existential and religious significance, and even from investigating the historical uniqueness of these phenomena in their particular contexts. This does not prevent us from adopting as a premise a universalistic basic model of the history of salvation and revelation. In other words, we may regard human history, wherever it contains valid religious elements, as always and everywhere the manifestation, not merely of a "natural" human religious disposition, but first and foremost an historical movement and energy which is the form in which God has always and everywhere inserted himself as the ultimate centre of reality.

A basic model of this sort does no violence to the "supernaturalness" of God's gracious self-communication, does not deny God's freedom with regard to the world. It simply demythologises in a legitimate way ideas of the history of salvation and revelation which inevitably predominate if the basic model of our understanding of this history is that of an action of God from outside which occurs only at specific distinct points. To this end, cautious demythologising corrections are possible in cases of individual religious phenomena so that they no longer appear incredible. We are not yet talking here about Jesus Christ, about how the absolute uniqueness and insurpassability of his person as the absolute bringer of salvation and of his work is to be preserved within the universalistic basic model, or even understood in the first place. Nor are we referring to the fact that for us too the Old Testament history of salvation and revelation can have and retain a particular and unique significance to the extent that it constitutes the immediate historical and religious context of Jesus Christ himself (one and a half millennia out of a history stretching over millions of years, all of which was also the history of salvation and revelation!). We are simply trying to make a little clearer how revelation in general is to be envisaged with this basic model.

The traditional view of the original bearers of revelation, the prophets, almost inevitably presents them as people who in some way had a particular private line to the God outside of the world in heaven and who passed on the messages which came down to them along this line to the rest of humanity. They also confirmed the correctness of the message they presented in this way by means of miracles. In other words, the traditional idea of the original bearer of revelation is marked in a special way by the particularistic and external basic model of an intervention of God from outside as a particular cause in the mechanism of the world. The fact that people today, as a result of the history of religions and the existence of many religions which all claim to be revealed, have great difficulties in imagining revelation in this way, is easy to understand. We find too many similar phenomena of religious revelation in the history of religion to feel able to set the Old Testament revelation apart from the rest of the history of religion as an absolutely unique phenomenon and the only one brought about by God in the strict sense. There is no clear boundary between real "prophets" and other religious geniuses and preachers. And the history of the Old Testament revelation contains scarcely any, indeed no, "miracles" of the sort required in the traditional theology of revelation to legitimate the bearer of revelation.

The history of Old Testament revelation seems to be historically conditioned and dependent on its context to such an extent that this provides no clear criterion, or none at all, for distinguishing it from other phases of the history of religion. If we nevertheless think we can discover in it unique peaks of religious consciousness, the question always remains whether this is not to be explained by the particular interest which we have in the Old Testament but not in other phenomena of religious history. It may also be the case that this uniqueness, if it is admitted, is no more than the inevitable peak of a history which does not always produce exactly the same phenomena. It is difficult to prove that a single phase or phenomenon in religious history is the sole event of revelation or exclusively the work of God, particularly since the actual course even of the history of a religion given uniquely privileged status as the sole history of revelation shows quite enough examples of human influence and depravity. We ourselves cut all this away, leaving the pure revealed religion which can then be clearly contrasted with other religions. It is we who make the contrast by reference to the religion and revelation of Jesus. Why this revelation should be not merely the provisional culmination of religious history, but its absolute summit even though the history of religion naturally continues, must be discussed later.

Leaving this question aside for the moment, we can make a number of points about the history of revelation in general. Insofar as God in his gracious self-communication always and everywhere offers himself to the unlimited openness of the human spirit in free and gracious self-disclosure, the authentic and grace-filled history of revelation in principle takes place always and everywhere, at least in the form of an offer. When, in the actual cultural history of the human race, this offer is not simply accepted in the subjectivity of an individual existence (automatically or inexplicitly, but really, which is always possible in any moral decision), but also given external form in social constructs (language, religious institutions and so on), we then have specific religions and their history. To the extent that these external forms do not essentially distort the true basic offer of revelation, namely God himself as the salvation of the human race, we can in principle, with regard to all these religions, speak of an element of divine revelation in the Christian sense.

These religions naturally always contain, in their specific lived form, inadequate and even wrong interpretations of the basic religious experience which is revelation, even of the most appalling and reprehensible kind, and it may be difficult to say in a specific case how far a particular religion is still conducive to that ultimate openness of a man or woman to the incomprehensibility of God. A particular religion, in its social and liturgical forms, always becomes a synthesis, which can never in the end be quite undone, between the authentic divine revelation at the core of human existence and everything which comes into being when this human divinity and divine humanity have their own history within general history, unfold and fade, bloom and seek their own perfection. This means that this history of the one divine self-revelation also includes phases of protest against abuses, phases of self-purification, of sublimation of its rites, of a deepening of reflection on its nature, and finally also, and especially, an encounter with other similar religious structures. In such an encounter a particular religion is also rightly faced with the vital question whether it must not transform itself, and develop into a higher form of religious life, a form which confronts it from another region of history and yet constitutes its own proper essence.

To repeat, we have not yet touched on the question of the uniqueness and unsurpassability of Christianity or, better, of Jesus Christ. But, leaving this question on one side, the enormous variety of the history of religion offers no ground for that tired scepticism which thinks that each religion can be taken on its own terms, because there are just too many and to make a choice between them is too difficult. The true and enormously important lesson to be learnt from the very multiplicity of religions is that human beings, wherever they are not stultified by a cult of triviality, search for the incomprehensible, the inexpressible, the sacred, as the ultimate fulfilment even of their own individual lives. This remains true even though, even in this ultimate longing of their existence, they constantly try to make use of this inexpressible object for their petty everyday ends. The fact that such deeply interior religion must also be a social religion should, despite all the consequences which this inevitably brings, be no argument against religion or a particular religion. It simply means (still ignoring Christianity as such) that a human being is quite right to live in confidence in the religion which seems most appropriate in the complexity of his or her historical, social and human situation. The person lives in the religion and through it performs that supportive surrender to the incomprehensible mystery which we call God and, to that extent at least, ultimately overcomes the difference of religions.

I have certainly not answered all the points the fifth enquiry raised, indeed in many cases I have not even tried to. What I have tried to do was simply to show that, in the attempt to understand the history of salvation and revelation it is ultimately possible, with all due caution and modesty, to do without a particularistic model of external intervention by God in his world at particular points of space and time, without having to interpret Christianity "naturalistically", in what used to be called a "modernistic" way. It reflects no honour on God if we limit his action to a few spatio-temporal conjunctions in the world and history. It is no denial of the enormous diversity which we find in history to say that it is always and everywhere God's history.

Six

Why Him?

Jesus of Nazareth is acknowledged by the Christian religion as the definitive prophet, the mediator and perfector of salvation history between God and human beings, the irrevocable self-revelation of God: in short, as the son of God made man. This is a very strange statement when you begin to reflect on it. And certainly too a declaration which creates false ideas in many people today. You yourself have written somewhere that a person of our time who has not already been brought up as a Christian must have a similar reaction to the Christian belief in the incarnation of God to ours when we are told that the Dalai Lama is the reincarnation of Buddha, in other words that it is pure mythology or, as most people would say, a "fairy tale". Which brings us to the enquiry underlying the remarks which follow: How can we tell that Jesus is more than other prophets or religious figures?

The only evidence we have about Jesus comes from people who already believed in him. We do not, so to say, have the "original" and it is, therefore, hard to discover who Jesus himself thought he was. But when I try to put myself in the place of a Jew of the time of Jesus, I can easily understand why he was rejected as the Messiah by the majority. The appearance of the Messiah was to mean the coming of the kingdom of God, in some sense the end of time. The Messiah was expected to confirm the law of Moses, not to call it into question. He was to enable the true religion of Israel to prevail over all pagan idolatry. Did that happen? The early Christians also believed that after the coming of the Messiah history really ought to stop. The "imminent expectation" of someone like Paul is a clear indication of this. My question is: Isn't Christianity here trying to get around two problems at the same time? First, the fact that the end of time did not come with Christ, and, second, the question of Jesus' knowledge: he proclaimed an imminent expectation which was not fulfilled. Did Jesus make a mistake? What did he really know? As God, he must have known everything, and even if we admit that his mission was not to satisfy human curiosity or to fill the gaps in secular knowledge by revelation, he was still wrong. And not just in his imminent expectation. Didn't Jesus believe also in the descent of all human beings from Adam and Eve? And why—which I find even worse— did he not protest with all the force at his command against the injustice of slavery? Are these questions simply to be left as unanswerable?

In fact, it is another question which I want to go into now in rather more detail. If we cannot accept the Dalai Lama as the reincarnation of Buddha, the reason is because there is nothing about him which sets him apart from other people and confirms his claim. But what confirms Jesus' claim? In the past, and in fact until recent times, people thought that there was confirmation of Jesus' claim in the fact that in him the prophecies of the Old Testament were fulfilled, that he did miracles and performed acts of power—and there is also the evidence of the "holiness" of the Church. The last point is something I don't want to talk about. It's hardly surprising that an authority which is itself judge of truth or error should always declare its own beliefs to be true. But what about the fulfilment of the prophecies? I can quite see that the primitive Christians of Jewish descent (and Christianity of course began as a Jewish sect) must have had the greatest interest in seeing the prophetic predictions fulfilled in Jesus Christ. But to us today the fulfilment of these prophecies sounds artificial and forced. What fitted was chosen and for the rest the rule was: delete the inapplicable.

And I'm not happy either about the miracles of Jesus. It is not at all the fact that extraordinary events took place as the result of Jesus' activity which makes me unhappy. It is much more my belief that extraordinary events have taken place in other places too, and still do today. The "exact sciences" cannot explain them, and they will probably never be able to explain them, because they are not regularly recurring, checkable phenomena. This is something science just has to face. Here I am ignoring Jesus' resurrection because this isn't a miracle like the others. But, accepting this, we must then exclude the miracle stories which have a clear sign character, that is, those which didn't happen at all, but were invented and used by the primitive community for catechetical purposes. Not as lies or fairy tales, of course, but to give symbolic expression to the activity of the Lord in his lifetime and in the time after his resurrection.

But what does this leave of the miracles? How many things, quite apart from Jesus, have been regarded as miracles which either have natural explanations or were not reinterpreted as events until later! So what confirms Jesus' claim to be the Son of God? I am not particularly impressed either by the fulfilment of the prophecies or by the miracles. So what about Jesus' teaching? I readily admit that Jesus of Nazareth was, in his short lifetime, certainly an honest, honourable, upright and religious man. A man who could not stand the legalistic religion of the Pharisees and scribes. Who dedicated himself to the poor, the deprived, to "sinners", and even forgave sins. But here again there's something that irritates me. Need this forgiving of sins have been more than the promise of a human being that God will forgive the sin of a person who repents? And furthermore need the connection, in which Jesus evidently believed, between himself and the coming of the kingdom of God have been more than an eschatological expectation of which there have been a great number (which have still not been fulfilled)? Allright. Even I know that theology can ask and answer such questions more subtly. But sometimes I am afraid that with all their abstruse speculations the theologians— consciously or unconsciously—are avoiding answering the simple questions which are nevertheless difficult ones, the "real" questions.

But now I've got off the point. What about Jesus' teaching

and message as proof of his divine origin? Jesus preached love, love even of enemies. No one will deny that this teaching ought to be a basic aim and a basic ideal of human life and human society. If only it were followed more the world would really be a much better place. And Jesus proclaimed love for human beings as love for him and at the same time love for God. Is this really so very special? So very special that it proves Jesus' divine origin? Isn't love between human beings always what religious people preach? Have the founders of other religions preached hatred? Must the proclamation of the unity of love of God and love of neighbour in itself prove the divinity of the proclaimer?

And again, I have no doubt about the historical uniqueness of Jesus as a person. I know very well that neither I nor millions of other people could achieve what Jesus achieved. My question is simply this: How do I get from the man Jesus of Nazareth to the God-man Jesus Christ? In the previous question I said already that the people of today have an immense fund of sympathy and admiration for Jesus. There are no polemics against Jesus—except on a level at which everything decent is mocked and made a target for the worst imputations. Everything I have mentioned so far, the honesty, integrity, uncompromising religious radicalism, the shattering effect of Jesus' message on his contemporaries (which continues to be felt today), the courage to die for the views he held: everyone readily admits that Jesus had all these qualities. All except the crucial one, being the Son of God. Where are the boundaries of what a human being can do but someone who is "only human" can no longer do?

I shall talk about Jesus' resurrection in the next enquiry. I say this because many parts of this enquiry can probably be answered only in that context, in the context of the resurrection. But the leap must not be taken too fast. After all, if Jesus' earthly life cannot prove what Jesus himself (according to the scriptures) said: "He who sees me sees the Father", even belief in the resurrection is little help; indeed it would be impossible. It would mean that the earthly Jesus was not the risen Christ—or that through the resurrection he had become something which, as a man, he neither was nor wanted to be.

To the question how they know that Jesus of Nazareth is the Son of God, the average Christian today will answer that Jesus' miracles prove that he was. I am not satisfied with this (even if the resurrection is included as a "miracle"). Exegetes have nibbled away too much, and modern science has robbed me of too many illusions, for that. I am not surprised that for this reason the traditional proofs of Jesus' divinity are no longer regarded as so important in the latest theology. It is now supposed to be Jesus' own teaching which proves him to have been the Son of God, or better, Jesus' teaching and life. This argument is based on the idea that a human being cannot but want particular "things", and that Jesus was the person who brought what we human beings—more or less explicitly—want. A human being, the argument runs, is a creature who all along is looking for Christ, who waits for him in history, as God's answer, either still awaited or already given, to the question a human being cannot avoid.

Here again I cannot escape two questions. First, what do human beings really want? (I touched on this problem in the first enquiry). Do they really want survival after death? Do they need more than a commitment, based on responsible hope, to a better (not the best possible) world? Do they need more than intellectual realisation that mutual love and consideration make for a better world than hatred, war and meanness? But above all, is the awareness of a fundamental correspondence between what human beings inevitably want and the teaching of Jesus a proof of Jesus' divinity? I mean, is it more than the admission that Jesus' teaching was "sensible", which by no means leads to accepting him as the incarnate God?

And the second point: Is it not striking that this view underplays what we Christians call the cross? Am I supposed to say that I always and necessarily want and look for that too? People say so lightly that the cross and suffering are inevitable, that they are stages on the way to eternal happiness, or that they are incomprehensible in their meaninglessness. Is that true? Isn't it, to put it as strongly as possible, an evasion, which tries to make the unintelligible intelligible, without facing the obvious objections which occurred to many Jews of Jesus' time (that a crucified Messiah is no Messiah and not the end of a constant human search)?

And so I ask once more: Where does the human being end when it takes God's infinity as its model? What can prove that a human being not only lives by this model more seriously and more faithfully than millions of others, but also is the self-revelation of God, and that means God himself in his fundamental nature?

*   *   *

Your sixth enquiry is concerned, as was to be expected, with Jesus Christ. It thereby introduces a subject of such breadth and complexity that I cannot possibly be expected to deal with it in a dozen pages with anything approaching adequacy, even if, as you suggest yourself, we leave Jesus' resurrection out of discussion for the moment. What I write on this subject can therefore be no more than a few remarks chosen almost at random, at the risk of leaving out what a reader may regard as much more important.

First of all, it seems to me, we Christians ought to be much more aware of the enormous demands on the courage and strength of our faith that are made by the Church's teaching about Jesus Christ. I cannot help feeling that the average preaching of this faith in the Church very often fails to meet the difficulty of this task either in quantity or quality. It usually just takes for granted the fundamental statements of the Church's Christology, instead of constantly trying to make them credible. Even in the Church a modern form of Jesuolatry is tempted to try and get round the fundamental statements of a dogmatic Christology by enthusiastically identifying with the human demands of Jesus and so again only responding to those elements in Jesus' message which correspond to its existing attitudes. On the other hand, I also have the impression that current Christology, simply because it knows that it is on orthodox lines, adopts too easy and naive an attitude to the language of the tradition. I can't help feeling that orthodox Christology simply passes on the traditional Christological formulas with the feeling that nothing in orthodox doctrine could ever get really unintelligible. I believe, however, that even a genuinely orthodox Christology has the duty to take great care that the proper burden of saving faith is not covertly increased by the addition of burdens deriving from the thoughtlessness and idleness of a pseudo-orthodoxy. Even in Christology, mystery and absurdity are not identical, but must be clearly distinguished. A modern "Christology from above" (however true it may be) may also not live covertly on a mythological and outmoded image of the world in which it was not particularly surprising that God should descend from heaven into his world. All this, however, should be taken as no more than a brief introduction.

As regards the subject of Jesus' miracles as evidence for the claims of his message and his understanding of himself, I suggest that we limit ourselves to the "miracle" of his resurrection and therefore postpone this topic to the next question. The "miracles", which Jesus performed in his earthly life and which certainly cannot be conjured away by a trivial historical rationalism, simply face us, historically and in substance, with too many problems for us to dispose of them in a quick burst of apologetics or use them as apologetic arguments. Indeed, it is not obvious in advance that each and every miracle, given that it was "in itself" a miracle, has or should have the same apologetic weight in every place and at every time.

Shall we get another point of disagreement out of the way in advance? I admit that Jesus, in his human consciousness, did not know everything and envisaged the end of the world in a way which, if we were to take it as immediately relevant to us and in our modern context, we would justifiably describe as mistaken. I know I am expressing myself in a rather complicated way. As far as I am concerned, anyone who wants to may quite happily say that Jesus "made a mistake" in his imminent expectation of the end of the world (or about the origin of all human beings from a single Adam). I would not accuse such a person of heresy, although I would not use such language myself. It obscures an existentially fundamental distinction between an opinion on the one hand without which, at a particular historical moment, a fundamental and enduring truth could not in practice have been understood by a particular person and, on the other hand, an opinion which, because existentially uninteresting, is simply incorrect or was recognisably incorrect even within such an existentially significant situation. I maintain that in the first case it is better to "make a mistake" and that this "mistake" should not be so called because in the situation described we are closer to authentic truth with this "mistake" than without it.

I should like to ask whether the conceptual model of an endless continuation of our history (which would then no longer be a history) brings us closer to the real truth of our existence than an "apocalyptic" conceptual framework of the sort within which Jesus expressed his imminent expectation. To put it briefly, Jesus expressed an imminent expectation which we find, whether we want to call it mistaken or not in the form it has for us, unfulfilled. On the other hand, such "error" is part of the historical nature of human existence, which we surely do not want to deny to Jesus. The fact that he "is" God and to that extent omniscient, has intrinsically as little to do with the issue of his human consciousness as if someone were to maintain that he holds the world in his human hand because he is omnipotent. It really does not shock me that Jesus did not demand the liberation of slaves, even if we assume that this problem did not explicitly concern him even at the deepest level of his consciousness. The consciousness of an individual human being is, after all, historically conditioned and limited. No individual human being's consciousness has the scope and responsibility of the total consciousness of the human race in its whole history. The idea that Jesus' consciousness was something like a universal encyclopaedia in innumerable volumes may have been widespread in medieval theology, but it is not compatible with belief in the true humanity of Jesus.

We must now get closer to the essence of Christology. First, Easter is part of the definition of Jesus; that is, the resurrection is not simply a confirmation of Jesus' message and his view of himself which remains external, but the whole significance of Jesus for our salvation cannot be just transferred to his resurrection alone, in a way which made it of no importance what sort of message Jesus had proclaimed in his earthly life and how he had thought of himself.

You ask in the sixth enquiry whether the teaching and the example of the earthly Jesus are really so unique and original and incomparable that they are themselves sufficient to confirm Jesus' understanding of himself or the theological interpretation of his identity as the only-begotten Son of God. The answer to this question is difficult because, if the weight is placed mainly on one side or the other (life–resurrection), the problem becomes insoluble. The truth is that Jesus' teaching and his understanding of himself do not ultimately prove their claim and, conversely, without them we would have no idea who it was that had risen; we would have either a letter without a seal or a seal without a letter. We must have an even closer look at what the real content and core of Jesus' preaching and understanding of himself is and how the content of his message and his own understanding of himself relate to each other. Another (or a prior) question is of course whether, how and to what extent we are able, with the resources of modern historical scholarship, to answer this question, that is, to know what the historical Jesus really preached and thought about himself.

With regard to all these questions we can say first of all that if Jesus simply preached and lived an obvious humanism, even if perhaps in a purity and impressiveness not found elsewhere, if he had in addition reinforced this by talking about a loving Father in heaven who bestowed sun and rain on just and sinners with equal benevolence, this would be neither a message which raised him above the level of a religious reformer or prophet in a still uncompleted series of such figures, nor could it explain why his message is inseparable from his person and allows conclusions to be drawn from it about his person. We orthodox Christians ought not to dismiss too quickly this sort of Jesuolatry in its diverse variants. It is a perfectly serious question whether a human being with an absolute and pure love without any egoism must not be more than a human being. If the moral personality of Jesus in word and life really makes such a compelling impression on a person that they find the courage to commit themselves unconditionally to this Jesus in life and death and therefore to believe in the God of Jesus, that person has gone far beyond a merely horizontal humanistic Jesuolatory and is living (perhaps not completely spontaneously, but really) an orthodox Christology.

However, orthodox Christology must give its own implications a thorough examination. We must, therefore, ask: Does there exist sufficiently secure historical knowledge of the content of Jesus' preaching and of his own understanding of himself to allow us to translate the content of Jesus' preaching and of his self-understanding into the classical Christology of the New Testament? The question of course assumes that the explicit content of this preaching and self-understanding of Jesus are not already expressed in the concepts and conceptual frameworks of classical (and indeed New Testament) Christology, but require translation. We naturally have every right to expect also that such a translation will not only confirm the classical Christology of the New Testament and the Church, but will also be capable of eliminating incorrect, exaggerated, quasi-mythological ideas, which quite often get mixed up with Christian teaching in current Christology.

So, what is the content of Jesus' preaching and of his own view of himself which makes both inseparably linked? In these few lines we can of course only answer this question with a sort of assertion, and cannot provide the detailed exegetical studies and evidence which would be strictly required.

Jesus proclaims the victorious coming of the kingdom of God, which is addressed to the "just" and sinners. It is not the fundamental characteristic of this victorious coming of the kingdom of God that in a literal sense it should come very quickly. It is true that the absolutely victorious character of this coming was imagined by Jesus in the form of a sudden arrival, and why not? Anyone who does not think of it in this way can always be asked whether they really seriously envisage this irrevocable coming. No, its fundamental characteristics are that it comes from God, that it comes in inevitable victory and transcends (without destroying) human freedom in the power of divine compassion, by which God approaches the sinful world in forgiveness.

The uniqueness of Jesus' preaching of the coming kingdom consists in the fact that Jesus has the courage to know how the enormous drama of world history, which rises out of the depths of God's freedom and human freedom, will finally end. God, to whom it could make no difference to be defeated in the history of the world by the malice of creaturely freedom because he was always the Lord and guarantee of this vile damnation in which the human race insisted on imprisoning itself, is in fact victorious in his mercy and love. The individual in the history of his or her freedom may never have the right to pass the final judgment of life and pardon upon his or her own history, but must accept his or her own freedom as open and threatened—but the history of this human world as a whole ends in God and not in the abandonment in which finitude and guilt never go beyond themselves and do not reach God.

This message of Jesus' of the victory of God's love achieved by God himself and by his power, in which God gives himself to the world, may appear obvious to self-confident men and women today. They may think that, as long as there is a God, no other outcome is possible than a victory of light and love. But if this optimism is based on human beings and not on God, this person is forgetting the appalling depths of human history, the depths of their own sin and capacity for sin. If this optimism has any basis or justification, it is not in any essential characteristic of human reality. It is God's grace in human beings which gives this firm hope, even if this grace is misunderstood as a self-evident human capacity and autonomous right. That history as a whole will have a victorious and happy ending, that the kingdom of God, by the power of God, will irrevocably and remorselessly come, is a message which we have no possible means of working out by our own resources. It is simply incredible that it can be proclaimed at all while history is still in progress since history radically alters the situation of human beings with regard to freedom, though without neutralising its responsibility and precariousness.

But we cannot go into this in more detail here. This is the message which Jesus proclaimed. Before we ask what this message implies in more specific terms about its bearer, we need to make our previous statement a little more accurate and complete. The historical Jesus proclaimed this message from the very beginning of his public activity, that is, at a time when he did not yet envisage the failure of his mission to Israel and his death. But (ignoring more complicated considerations) his message, with its claim on our faith, comes to us only across his death and his resurrection, and we need have no qualms about including his fate in the content of his message for us. If he had not maintained his conviction of the victory of the kingdom of God through his death, if his faith as a belief in this coming of God had not remained victorious where everything is destroyed in death, if he had remained in death and not "risen", his message would have no claim on us, would not exist for us. The outcome of his life, which is completed in his victorious death, is itself part of his message of the victory of the kingdom of God. (This really ought to be explained in more detail, but there is no more room here; the main thing that needs to be shown is that, while the world remains sinful, an ultimate, absolutely radical faith which is an acceptance of the kingdom of God and of his message is possible only through death, in which everything that is not God is destroyed.)

In Jesus God has promised himself to the world in a way which will ultimately be victorious. God is not only the basis of a history of human freedom and does not merely support it in its own power; he does not simply offer himself to this history of freedom as its eternal perfection; he has not only (as we know through Jesus) had from all eternity the secret desire to have the last word in this history of freedom, not by abolishing it but through the prevenient power of his love. His method is to bring about (from the deepest centre of this world and of the history which he himself is) in this history an event which both itself expresses this divine world and history and makes it irreversible and also is its revelation. This saving event which reveals and makes victoriously present in the world God's definitive saving will, the event in which God "commits" himself, cannot be simply a creaturely reality different from God, existing in infinite separation from God. If it were no more than this, it would always be ambivalent, and could not firmly commit the infinite freedom of God. It would always remain (even if understood as an "expression" of God) subject to an ultimate qualification.

If a finite, creaturely reality is really to be the irreversible self-expression of God, which commits God himself, it must have a different relation to God from that of being merely his creation. The connection between this utterance which expresses God himself and fixes him in the world and God may be very difficult to put, even inadequately, into words, but a human being who wants to take hold of the miracle of this divine self-commitment triumphantly and victoriously cannot avoid this intellectual effort. In the attempt a person may, on the one hand, not eliminate the enduring difference between "God in himself" and the utterance by which he promises himself definitively to the world; and on the other hand a person may not envisage the distinction in the way it normally holds between God and a creature, because, if the "utterance" or "expression" were conceived as a merely finite creation, the difference would be so great that it could never be in itself an irreversible self-expression.

The more precise expression of this desired understanding is a problem which has been constantly preoccupying Christianity for almost 2000 years, and despite the results of these efforts, which are very good and have the status of official church teaching, it would be wrong to say that they had produced, or could produce, a result which from now on could simply be handed down in a definitively fixed formula, with nothing more necessary. (In passing, let me mention, though I cannot develop the idea here, that the conceptual problem of Christology with regard to the joining of God and humanity in a unity which leaves the difference unimpaired but keeps the unity intact, which transcends the difference between God and creature, also exists essentially, though in a modified form, with regard to God's union with his creature through the bestowal of his own spirit and with regard to the direct vision of

God.) In this traditional effort the union of Jesus with God, which makes him merely the irreversible and historically accessible word of God's promise of himself to the world, is usually presented as the "incarnation" of God (of the divine Logos) in a hypostatic union. Since this incarnation of God cannot be envisaged as the transformation of God into a human being, which would be sheer nonsense, it may be understood only as a unifying assumption of human reality alongside God's own reality.

When it is then asked how the unity between the divine and human realities so produced is to be envisaged so as not to remove the distinction between the two, the answer is given that this union is such that human realities can genuinely be attributed to the divine Logos who unites this human reality to himself: God is a human being, was born, died, and so on. Without thereby wishing to doubt the correctness and religious importance of these traditional answers to the question of the "hypostatic union", we can ask a further question about how these propositions ("is-propositions") are to be understood more precisely. It is clear that this "is" cannot identify the notion contained in the subject of the proposition (God) with the notion contained in the predicate (human being, being born, and so on) in the same way as other propositions with which we are familiar. This allows us to draw the conclusion that the statements about the incarnation of God through the hypostatic union are correct and legitimate because they express a particular unique relation between Jesus and God, which is not less but greater than the difference between God and creature, though of course it does not eliminate it.

However, the assertion of the incarnation of God in the hypostatic union itself in turn raises a question of understanding which cannot be simply suppressed with an appeal to religious mystery. It is not critical rational questions from outside which raise this question of understanding, but the dogma of the enduring difference between divinity and humanity in and despite the hypostatic union. This dogma itself asks how the union is to be understood, if the "is" which expresses this union is not to be confused with the normal "is" of an identifying proposition and if the danger of identification is inherent not merely in reasoning, but also in religion.

This problem of understanding obviously cannot be solved by another speculative exploration, but only by going back once more to our understanding of Jesus himself and his mission. This means that the incarnation and the hypostatic union must be interpreted in such a way as to bring out the meaning of the prior statement that Jesus, in what he was, his life, his death and his resurrection, and his message (altogether), is God's irreversibly victorious promise of himself to the world and as such historically accessible. What we are trying to say is that on the one hand the assertion of the incarnation of the Logos and the hypostatic union is a fully legitimate, intelligible, and in the long run unavoidable (as something like a transposition into a metaphysical interpretative framework) statement, with the authority of the Church's official teaching, about the prior religious assertion of the irreversible arrival of God himself among us in Jesus. On the other hand, however, the possibility of a religious experience of Jesus which is in some way prior to this "metaphysical" Christology gives us a specifiable source of religious knowledge and a criterion by which to judge "metaphysical" Christology.

Purely in passing, let me say that such a view also has implications for preaching. A preacher may not console himself with the thought that his Christological preaching will inevitably fail, and that it doesn't matter if he does not get through to the people of our time with the formula, "God is (became) man". He has complete freedom, and the duty, to say the same thing in a different way, though he must try to get his hearer to understand that the truth of Jesus is properly expressed in one way in the official teaching of the Church, but that he himself is required and allowed to explain this truth in a different way. If the statement "God is man" fills people with a metaphysical giddiness which paralyses their religious energy, then they should simply say firmly: In Jesus God has promised himself to me completely and irrevocably. This promise can no longer be revised or cancelled in spite of the infinite possibilities which God has at his command. He has appointed an end to the world and its history and that end is himself, and this decree is not merely present in God's eternal thoughts, it has already been inserted into the world and history by God himself, in Jesus who was crucified and rose again. Anyone who says this believes precisely what the Church's metaphysical Christology is trying to tell him or her with the ontology and logic of the hypostatic union and the communication of idioms, which are an attempt to protect us from false delusions and reinterpretations. That is what they are saying, not "more", because anything more would be a straying into mythology.

Allow me to write a sort of supplement to the sixth enquiry in short sections. I am not quite sure what we are supposed to imagine by the reincarnation of Buddha in the Delai Lama. Jesus is certainly not the reincarnation of another human being, and so the comparison between him and the Dalai Lama automatically fails. If and insofar as the historical Buddha succeeded, by eliminating all self, in experiencing the infinite, inscrutable fulness of divinity, the "nothing" of the finite, however he spontaneously interpreted and expressed this experience, he would have been simply an anonymous Christian saint. But I have no means of knowing whether this was really his situation or whether it endured through death to the definitiveness of his free existence. I have no means of knowing, because he did not identify himself with me and all other sinners, whether his merely hypothetical final fate means a promise of salvation for me. I have no means of knowing whether God's action, which in the end is the only thing we can rely on, guarantees that God will reach me, quite apart from all contemplative techniques. In short, as far as I am concerned, Buddha could be a saint, perhaps a prophet, but not the irreversible word of God's promise of himself to me.

That such a word of promise is the absolute mystery of the fact that God himself can come to me, that this possibility can be announced as a victorious reality among us in human history, that it is definitively announced to us in Jesus, all this is certainly the impenetrable mystery of the incomprehensible God. Nevertheless it is believable because it is what we hope for, and has nothing at all to do with mythology, unless we automatically sloppily call anything mythology that goes beyond trivial everyday experience. The previous remarks about the teaching and message of Jesus, which were an attempt to make them relevant for a religious understanding of the person of Jesus, concentrated on his announcement of the inevitable coming of the kingdom of God, because there at least we have a definite feature of his teaching. It is held against him, as the so-called mistake of his imminent expectation, but it is easier to see its Christological relevance than that of his humanism of selflessness and love. This is not to insist that all the other contents of his preaching (which are intimately connected and mutually define each other) have no such importance for Christology, but to remark that, because of the limits of space, we cannot here discuss other elements (such as, for example, his claim of power to forgive sins, which was certainly unique in his world).

Our remarks so far have avoided dealing with the problem raised by the sixth enquiry under the heading of Jesus' position as the "Son of God". The reason for this is that this term contains an enormous number of intrinsic and historical difficulties which we cannot attempt to resolve within the limits of this book. It cannot be denied that Jesus had a particular unique relationship with God, whom he called his Father, and that he did not ascribe this unique relationship in a simple way to any other person. No less can it be denied that this unique relationship of Jesus with God can be called "sonship", which distinguishes us, the "servants", from him. But the further proposition that this relationship itself in turn rests on a sonship within God deriving from a generation of this Son by the Father within God is a combination of statements from the theology of the Trinity which, correctly understood, are an essential part of the Christian faith, but which do not need to be examined here when we are dealing with such fundamental problems of faith as the ones we have been given.

Towards the end the sixth enquiry alludes to what might be called, in academic theological jargon, transcendental Christology, a Christology of searching. We cannot of course here outline a theory of man (in philosophical terms and with the covert theological implications inherent in the unavoidable effects of grace on human beings). This, however, is what would be required to show that human beings are not simply "hearers of the word", who must listen for such a word of God in their history, but also creatures who must listen in search of an all-embracing word of promise from God in history. Is such a theory of man inherently nonsensical? Can human beings automatically reject it in tired boredom with a cheap scepticism? Are human beings as such really tolerable even if their characteristics really became fixed and final as a result of some radical force? No, human beings are looking for themselves with infinite demands, and in Jesus, who was crucified and rose again, they take hold of a confirmation of this claim which is advancing to victory, a claim without which they would suffocate. When we are told that facts prove that human beings can certainly manage quite well without these demands, provided they are given a little happiness, that is an appeal, either to human beings who have so far failed to discover the limits of the prison of their finitude, or to human beings behind whose sceptical modesty an infinite hope is really alive, though they dare not admit it. You ask sceptically in your question whether such a Christology of searching which starts from our point of view also seeks the cross? A difficult question. Obviously such a Christology of seeking, in which human beings as the question are still looking for the God-man as the answer, cannot set out to deduce the actual life of Jesus *a priori*. Nevertheless, when we bear in mind the actual conditions of our existence as they are, it seems to me that such a Christology of searching can certainly discover death as a necessary element in the answer it is looking for.

God's victorious promise of himself to the human race can be a victorious promise only when it appears in a human being as definitively accepted and accessible. I do not presume to say that a Messiah victorious before his death would automatically be no Messiah. But may I not say that the Messiah, God's irrevocable promise of himself to the world, which is a definitive promise only when it is definitively accepted by human beings, can be what it is only through death? Everything before death is provisional, open to revision, a stage, after which others can be expected indefinitely. The scandal of the cross, death as a breakthrough into definitiveness in the form of an incomprehensible and total failure, must not be explained away. But even if this too is impermissible, we are by no means forbidden to imagine that in the actual situation of our existence acceptance of God's promise of himself, an acceptance which alone makes the promise victorious and takes it beyond mere words, can only take place both freely and finally in and through death.

Jesus, in the unity of his teaching, his life, his death and his resurrection is the historically accessible, irreversible presence of God's promise of himself to the world. Jesus himself understood himself in this way in his preaching of the coming of the kingdom which can no longer be stopped. If this is our picture of Jesus, then˙ he is certainly not just a religious reformer, a prophet in an unended series of prophets succeeding each other and perhaps also each going a little bit further than the other, but an absolutely unsurpassable, unique event in the history of salvation and revelation. If this is our picture of him, he is the one professed by the Christian belief in the doctrine of the incarnation and the hypostatic union. Because in this traditional doctrine God and man are not "confounded" into a third entity through the hypostatic union, but this union becomes intelligible only when we go back to the experience of salvation history that this Jesus is God's final word to us, the doctrine of the hypostatic union, of God's becoming human, has no mythological overtones which could make it incredible. The event of God's promise of himself in Jesus makes that deepest promise by God of himself to the world historically accessible and irreversible. It is always and everywhere the fundamental energy and force of the world and its history. It is therefore perfectly possible to understand the event of Jesus without the aid of images of an intervention by God in the world from outside. In doing without such an image, however, we must let history really be history and clearly realise that this deepest energy and power of the world and its history is God in his sovereign freedom, who, by his free promise of himself, has made himself this deepest energy and force of the world.

This perhaps needs a little getting used to, but even Jesus, insofar as he is "God himself among us", does not have to be thought of as that mysterious gardener who, without our noticing, climbs over the fence that runs around our world. A Christian can and should without worrying, profess and pray: "He came down from heaven", though in this case the statement and the conceptual model are not simply identical. However, when we say at the same time that the God-man was conceived by the Holy Spirit, this is the Spirit of God who has been poured out all along over all flesh as the love which has always powerfully moved the world.

Seven

Redemption and resurrection

Jesus' death on the cross is an historical fact. Despite its appalling horror, a few decades later after the destruction of Jerusalem thousands of Jews died in the same way, and death in wars and concentration camps was and is certainly no more pleasant. The way Jesus died is not the important thing—though it is interesting to consider whether it would have been different if Jesus had died at an appropriate age and not in his youth, say from a heart attack. The important point is that the death of the incarnate Son of God is our redemption—redemption from inherited guilt and personal sin. It was in this way that the "gate of heaven" was once more opened, the gate to that heaven into which God's saving plan had called us from the very beginning. Jesus, so the Christian faith teaches, expiated our sins by his death. He made satisfaction to God, and only a satisfaction adequate to God—that is satisfaction made by his Son, that is, in some way by God himself—could cancel out the offence done to God by the sins of human beings. Only the expiatory death of God could satisfy God.

But somewhere the equation doesn't work out. Human sins, the fact of which I do not doubt, are supposed to have caused God "infinite" offence. That may be, but if so why cannot human sorrow, repentance and amends be an "infinite" satisfaction for God? This is simply confusing or displacing levels. We can illustrate this by an idea which is admittedly absurd. If the God-man had sinned, then satisfaction by a God-man would make sense. However, if only human beings, if only we are the sinners, why then should satisfaction by the God-man be required?

And if nevertheless that is the way it had to be (even if I cannot see why), isn't this death of Jesus an expiatory sacrifice which is really unworthy of a loving God and Father? Ought there not to have been a different way, less cruel and more merciful? And another point comes in here. Is there an equivalence between Jesus' crucifixion and human sin? There is no need to minimise in any way the malice and duplicity of which human beings are capable. There is no need to explain away by psychology all responsibility until the greatest viciousness is no longer wrong, but merely a curiosity for depth psychology. But even without doing this is the guilt of the human race or of individual human beings so great that it can be expiated in no other way than by the divinely willed expiatory death of an innocent person, his own Son, on the cross?

What image of God is behind the process of redemption? I can find only the face of a God who punishes, the God of revenge. An eye for an eye, a tooth for a tooth. This may have been the image of the Old Testament God, but as far as I can see it is not that of the God Jesus proclaimed. Certainly, if I could see that redemption were possible only in this way, by Jesus' expiatory death, it would be easier. It would be easier to celebrate the adoration of the cross, of the death and agony of Jesus, as we Christians do every Good Friday. And I really don't want to attack the crucifixes in our Christian houses. The fact that we are redeemed by the crucifixion of Jesus is certainly the teaching of holy scripture and of our faith, and not even a non-Christian, as far as I can see, could fail to be impressed by the trust and confidence with which Jesus accepted his death. Only, I would like to understand, perhaps understand a little better, what the theologians call the "theory of satisfaction", the doctrine of making amends for human guilt.

And here there is something else which worries me, which I am reluctant to mention because I can imagine how difficult it must be to answer. But then it was agreed that difficulty should not be a reason for excluding questions that worry people today. One of these questions is hell, something which comes up in connection with the subject of redemption. An ex-Christian writes in a book about hell (I am only giving a rough summary): If a hell existed, what point would it have? In contrast to human prisons, any hope of the re-education of the people being punished is excluded. Hell is eternal. Repentance and sorrow are no longer possible. The only logical conclusion is that God wants to punish human beings, and so we are brought face to face once more with a God of revenge, not the God of love and forgiveness.

What can one say to such an argument? Another point is that we may well ask whether there can be human guilt so great as to justify the appalling torments and sufferings of an eternal, never-ending hell of separation from God. So is hell only scaremongering? A pious lie to make believers remember that their faith is to be taken seriously? I can't imagine that. The opposite view has as much truth: If hell does not exist, and if we could be certain of this, then our acts and omissions would lose any moral seriousness, they would be a game, and not decisions about (eternal) life and (eternal) death! How does the Christian escape this dilemma?

One last point on this subject of redemption, about this world, not the next. Where do we Christians really feel redeemed? What has redemption changed? The accusation (as far as I remember, it comes originally from Nietzsche) that Christians ought to look more redeemed if anyone was to believe in their redeemer, is not just an idle remark. The joy of redemption, the joy of freedom cannot be seen in the faces of most Christians. One could wish for a little more external manifestation of the knowledge of redemption in the Church as a whole, a little more of what, say, John XXIII radiated.

And now on the subject of the resurrection. Here, once more, I am rather at a loss. There was a time when every effort was made (and all sorts of stupid arguments were used) to disprove the event of the resurrection. It was all said to be a fraud by the disciples, mass hallucination, disappointment which had to or wanted to make up for the "real event" (i.e., the non-resurrection), and so on. This is understandable.

People automatically reject the idea of the resurrection of a dead person.

My problem with the resurrection of Jesus is not primarily a theological argument or a matter of faith. It's more a question about psychology. As a Christian, what should I do, what can I do, if, in spite of everything, a suspicion remains that somehow something is or could be "rotten" with the whole business? Is it inconceivable that, through a combination of all the possible factors (of which we know nothing) the disciples on the one hand believed in the risen Lord, but on the other the resurrection did not in fact really take place. Perhaps you will reply that this is another case which depends on attitudes, which shouldn't be automatically accepted. And perhaps you will also refer me to experts in psychology. But even so I can still ask: Don't you sometimes feel the same? Don't you too feel the remains of a lingering scepticism? And if so what do you do? What would you advise? What advice would you give to people who cannot work out any arguments against the belief in the resurrection, and yet regard it as a demand on their credulity which they simply can't accept?

To end with, let me mention one or two things which are connected with questions of belief in the resurrection. One thing must strike everybody: Why did Jesus appear only to those who subsequently believed in his resurrection? Why, in other words, are the resurrection appearances limited to the group of people who (apart from Paul) already had a close relationship with the earthly Jesus? Jesus' resurrection would be much more credible if, as the risen Lord, he had shown himself to his enemies and opponents, or at least to the many who regarded him, perhaps not as the possible Messiah, but at least as a prophet. Wouldn't belief in the resurrection be easier if Jesus had appeared to other people as well as his disciples and apostles? Of course the principle that we can't lay down rules for God applies here too, though the question that is touched on here conceals another problem.

Is it really as absurd as some theologians claim that the disciples' belief in the resurrection of the Lord might be only a mythological statement? That is, a statement which expresses belief in Jesus being with God, but uses words which suggest a real, to exaggerate, tangible and physical resurrection? Mythology—it was common at that time. Existential experiences, intense beliefs, were portrayed as historical facts, but were not intended as such, and this was known and understood by the people of the time. So the message of the resurrection would mean no more than "The cause of Jesus goes on". If I take this argument further I can say, if this were true, the situation we have described would be easier to understand, that is, the fact that Jesus appeared only to his disciples. The disciples may nevertheless, after a period of understandable disappointment, have come to the firm belief that the message of the earthly Jesus, his "cause", had to go on, had to go on being preached—and this, in the language of that time, was expressed in the word "resurrection". This need not have any effect on the fact of the resurrection itself. Only, the basis of the faith of Christianity would then be weaker, if there were nothing more than the subjective beliefs of the disciples and apostles of Jesus. But subjective beliefs are just like that. They may be false, without bad intentions, without a desire to trick or deceive.

* * *

The seventh enquiry deals with the death of Jesus in its aspect as (alleged) redemption of the world from its sin and with the resurrection of Jesus. These two topics, despite all their connections, which have been discussed above, can be quite clearly distinguished and so can also be clearly treated one after the other. I hope I shall therefore be allowed to reverse the order and start with Jesus' resurrection because it is only with regard to Jesus' complete life history that we can ask what its significance is for the redemptive event of salvation which took place in Jesus Christ.

How should one begin a theological consideration of the reality and meaning of Jesus' resurrection? There are of course many such possible starting points, and the one I choose here does not claim to be more than one possibility among many. Do I wish for my resurrection? I would probably not ask this question in this form, in these terms, if the doctrine of the resurrection of Jesus and the resurrection of the dead did not exist. However, this makes no difference to the fact that I can ask this question, and have a right to, because other vital questions also often begin in practice with an experience which is in some way accidental. So, I say that I have a right and an obligation to wish for my resurrection. This wish exists implicitly always and everywhere, provided that I seriously maintain that my existence has an ultimate meaning and do not let it drop, in an unadmitted despairing scepticism, into the meaninglessness of nothing.

This assertion naturally depends on what I imagine "resurrection" to mean. If, on the one hand, I follow an intellectual tradition which goes back to the ancient Greeks and make a distinction between body and soul, such that the question of the final fate of these two parts expects two answers, then naturally it is impossible to maintain that the demand for a definitive form and a saving of my existence also implies what is meant by resurrection. If, however, despite all possible distinctions between body and soul, the fundamental premise for me and my existential experience of myself is the unity of my physical and mental existence, then for me the irrevocable claim that my existence shall be saved and acquire definitive form implies a claim to resurrection. In this connection it makes no difference in the end that I cannot imagine or portray the definitiveness of this existence as it also includes bodiliness.

In my view, it is a mistake to think that the actual definitive form of a human being is really easier to imagine in terms of his or her "soul", than if, while accepting all the legitimate distinctions of different elements, one regards a human being as a single entity. If one has a radical hope of attaining a definitive identity and does not believe that one can steal away with one's obligations into the emptiness of non-existence, one has already grasped and accepted the resurrection in its real content. It then no longer matters so much how we described this "physical" side of our total human definitiveness at the end of the history of our freedom. Various other problems also lose their importance: how we imagine the connection between this "physical" side of our total definitiveness and the "body" which we leave behind in death, whether we can imagine our own resurrected body existing without including the physical matter of our old body, which, of course, in death will have been abandoned to a process of total decay.

It is wrong to say that to develop an understanding of the resurrection in these terms is to practise rationalism on a dogma of faith. The absoluteness of the radical hope in which a human being apprehends his or her total existence as destined and empowered to reach definitive form can quite properly be regarded as grace, which permeates this existence always and everywhere. This grace is revelation in the strictest sense. Moreover, the Christian dogma of the resurrection of Jesus and, as an effect of this resurrection the resurrection of the dead, entails not just the definitiveness of human existence through deatħ, which would leave it quite uncertain whether the completed history of freedom ended with God or in definitive frustration. On the contrary, it says that, through the power of God, this history of freedom, in Jesus and in the human race, does in fact reach victory. However, this certainly is revelation, even if this is not envisaged as coming from "outside".

The resurrection I hope for is not a miraculous additional prize, not something I could modestly decline even while accepting the remorselessly radical quality of the responsibility implied in my history of freedom, but something which is an inevitable part of the interpretation of my existence imposed on my freedom. It is as such a creature that I hear Christianity's message of the resurrection of Jesus. It naturally contains more than the conviction that no human being, not even Jesus, has a chance of escaping into an empty void. The message of Jesus' resurrection says in addition that his definitive identity, the identity of his bodily history, has victoriously and irreversibly reached perfection in God. It ways that (also) this resurrection is God's promise to the world, that the whole history of the world too (without prejudice to the openness of each individual's history of freedom) certainly and irreversibly reaches its perfection in Jesus' Easter. Is such a message incredible?

Is the message incredible because it was given only to believers? We have to be very careful with this objection. Given
the nature of the case and the nature of the religious experience, there can be only two reactions to the experience of Jesus'
resurrection. Either one accepts the experience in faith and
recognises the resurrection of Jesus as having taken place, or
one denies the experience itself. The third possibility of accepting the experience and at the same time denying the content of
the experience does not exist; a no to the content is or becomes
necessarily a no to the experience itself. How could it be otherwise if belief in the resurrection of Jesus as a saving event is to
be free faith? The basis of faith can ultimately be thought of in
no other way than as something arrived at in faith itself, and
yet within this faith it provides a real basis. (This is also the case
with other ultimate existential human experiences: the meaning of love can be understood only by people who love. In love,
love carries its own justification and does not have to look for a
justification from outside itself. This also follows from the very
nature of the experiences we are talking about. If the free and
definitive identity which a person acquires in and through
death were to show itself outside the sphere in which a person
strains towards this definitiveness, the definitiveness would be
changed back into something provisional, still ambivalent and
in the process of becoming.)

Does the evidence of the first witnesses make the resurrection of Jesus incredible? They underwent the experience of the
resurrection as people who had given up all hope, as people
who were perfectly able to distinguish what they experienced
on the one hand and mystical or imaginative visions, hallucina-
tions on the other hand, even those to which they attributed a
positive religious significance. This experience of the first disciples, which they sustained with their loyalty until their deaths
and which is thereby shown to be different in kind from passing enthusiasm, may be difficult for us to analyse or classify. We
certainly should not imagine it in terms of the way spatio-
temporal realities of this world confront us in our everyday
experience. Such a picture would not show deep faith; it would
simply be wrong. Nor is there anything to stop us distinguish-

ing different elements in this experience, even if in the end they are inseparable.

May one of these elements be a hidden but real prior knowledge of a prophet's fate ending with a return, which makes the choice of the conceptual model "resurrection" for Jesus' final victory more intelligible? Is an experience of the empty tomb one of the original elements of the resurrection experience, or is it an inference from it? How far are the stories of appearances of the risen Jesus part of the original resurrection experience, and how far are they attempts to give dramatic form to an underlying experience? In my opinion we can ask these and other questions, and perhaps not be able to answer them very clearly, and yet have no hesitation in sharing the first disciples' belief in the resurrection.

In a unique experience, which is therefore very difficult to describe, the disciples found a certainty that Jesus, in the historical bodiliness of his life, was not destroyed but was alive and by his power gave them an active experience of this victorious definitiveness of his existence. Nor is this simply and solely the experience of the first disciples. Although we ourselves may always remain dependent on the testimony of the first disciples in order to be able to connect our experience of the spirit explicitly and by name specifically with Jesus, we may nevertheless say with confidence that wherever and whenever we experience the unshakeableness of our own hope of a final victory of our existence, there takes place, perhaps anonymously, that is, without reference to the name of Jesus, an experience that he has risen. For this power of the spirit that we experience in this way as life's victorious defiance of all forms of death is the power of the Spirit which raised Jesus from the dead and thereby displays its victorious power to the world in history.

But for the same reason the opposite argument is also valid. If the evidence of the first disciples together with the whole history of the Christian faith bears witness to us about the message of Jesus' resurrection, can we sceptically dismiss this message without also denying our own hope of resurrection? We have already said that the message of Jesus' resurrection says more than the individual ever hopes for himself or herself alone when he or she protests against a final disappearance of their personal and bodily existence in death. But, in the face of the life and death of Jesus, the difficulty of believing in Jesus' resurrection is not that it is uncertain or difficult to believe that this life is finally perfected in the light and in the love of the infinite God *if* it is not simply destroyed by death. It lies rather in the difficulty of this "if". This is where his and our fates meet. This is why we can and must certainly say that an attitude of sceptical indifference towards the question of his resurrection is also sceptical and despairing indifference towards the final self-assertion of our own existence.

We come now to the second point of the seventh enquiry. What does it mean more precisely, and how far is it credible, when we say that we are redeemed by he death of Jesus?

In discussing this question it must first be realised that for human beings the particularity of their history cannot be freely accepted only when this history has been shown to be necessary. We therefore cannot counter the story of the redemption with arbitrarily constructed alternative models (which perhaps seem to make sense and to be non-contradictory only in our heads) and suggest that the salvation of the world might just as well have been brought about by our plans. The question to be asked here is not whether something else might have been, but whether what is can be understood to some extent as meaningful and is therefore acceptable without absolute protest.

If we are objective and honest we must admit that the Christian doctrine of the redemption, as contained in the New Testament (redemption by the sacrifical blood of Jesus) and as presented in medieval theology (the theory of satisfaction), is not easy for us to understand today. It smacks of mythology because in a sphere which is not accessible to us relations of cause and effect are postulated and constructed, and distinctions are made where we can no longer make distinctions. An angry God, insisting on reparation for the offence done to him, becomes a forgiving God as a result of a bloody sacrifice by his own Son. The theory of satisfaction (which has never been defined as the official teaching of the Church) then presupposes that the sins of the world are an infinite offence because it measures them by the dignity of the person offended and not by that of the offender. It then assumes that the satisfaction made by Christ is of infinite value because satisfaction is measured by the dignity of the person making satisfaction, and that this satisfaction, which is made to the divine Trinity (and not merely to the Father) makes sense because of the difference between humanity and divinity, although the ultimate agent of this work of redemption and the basis of its infinite value is of course the divine Logos.

There is also the fact that this whole work of redemption, which is supposed to placate God and make him merciful, is the result all along of God's spontaneous desire to save, so that we must (also) clearly say, the saving work of Jesus Christ exists because even before it God was the God who forgives and triumphs over the sins of the world, and not (only) that God is merciful because of the saving work of Christ. Indeed a Christian who is worried and perplexed by the dreadfulness of the sins of the world, which God does permit together with their further consequences, may think that the holy and merciful God only allowed an evil to enter this world which all along was encompassed by a will which was to triumph over it, in which God's Yes to the world prevails even over the No of human freedom.

But if all this is true, how can we still say that we are redeemed by the blood of Christ, by his sacrifice, by the satisfaction which he made for us to God's holy righteousness? How are we to understand such statements if God's will to prevail as grace over the No of the creature is the cause and not ultimately the result of what happened on the cross? We cannot make things easy for ourselves by saying simply that what happened on the cross convinces us of God's desire to save and so arouses in us belief in God's offer of salvation. This answer is also correct, and contains a truth of fundamental importance for anyone who does not have a superficial view of God as a good person whose job is obviously forgiving. Yet this answer on its own obviously doesn't do justice to the traditional Christian beliefs about the saving work of Christ. One element of Christ's saving work must be its influence on God, even if this "on" must be qualified in all sorts of ways in order not to obscure the unapproachable sovereignty of God and his will.

We may first ask formally: Are there events which can be regarded both as the effects of a will and also as its "cause"? We may say that if and insofar as a will has to implement itself (itself!) by bringing about something other than itself in which it expresses itself (itself!) and becomes definitive, then this objectifying expression of this will is not only an effect, but also a cause of this will insofar as that will would not really have existed in its ultimate seriousness and irreversibility if this expression had not existed. A murder is more than a wish to murder and a wish to murder would not be really and radically itself if it was not realised and expressed in a real murder. The fact that the intention to murder as carried out also depends on conditions which do not depend on the wish alone makes no difference to this. God's will from the beginning was to forgive and sanctify sinful human beings and it is present and active always and everywhere in the world as grace. In guiding the history of the world as its own it exists no longer merely as an offer to human freedom in the world, but clearly prevails and in this victory transcends the ambivalence of God's offer to freedom and becomes historically accessible. It becomes accessible in such a way that what is at first an individual victory is also the promise of victory by the power of God to mankind as a whole. In these circumstances such an event is both the action of this spirit of God in the world and also the "cause" of this victory insofar as in the victory the Spirit is bringing its own history to a victorious and irreversible end.

This is just what happened in the death and resurrection of Jesus understood as a single saving event. The victorious death is not a private event in the life of Jesus inasmuch as it, as an act of God, is initiated by the will with which God wills the salvation of the world as a whole. From Jesus' point of view this death is a universal saving event in that Jesus does not abandon his solidarity with the sinful human race even in death. In this victorious death the grace of God now becomes irreversible in the world and manifest in history (resurrection!).

What we have here is not just a human being who, through a death accepted without reserve, himself found God's freedom. That much we may hope from the death of every human being in the long history of the human race. But that the death of some other person means for me a promise from God himself, that we can know in faith of no other death than that of Jesus. For, in the case of other people, how can we know that they are dying in solidarity with me, that they (and this is a bold statement) wish to obtain their salvation from God's incomprehensibility only if and insofar as this wish means me too and not just them? Of what other human being, except precisely of Jesus, can we know in faith that the surrender of death was an act of unconditional trust and not an ultimate despair at the disappearance of all support? Where, except in Jesus' resurrection, can I find the certainty that this capitulation is nothing other than the victorious outcome of his death, victorious for us in history (even if in its end) and therefore accessible, an outcome which in all other cases remains questionable? His victorious death is the fulfilment and the victorious appearance of this fulfilment makes God's saving will, always and everywhere at work in the world, irreversible. As the historical manifestation of this fulfilment, the death of Jesus is both the effect and also the cause of the grace in which God is always and everywhere the deepest energy and force of salvation history.

This is a more precise and circumscribed definition of the causality of the cross in its relation to God's saving will, but it can quite properly be expressed also in the traditional conceptual frameworks, provided that one realises all the time that this whole event of the cross derives totally from God's merciful will to communicate himself, which has no other cause than God himself.

This description certainly provides the basis for a correct— certainly one more correct than the usual one—interpretation of the working of redemption. People often ask if things have got better in the world since we have been redeemed by the cross of Christ. They assume that since the cross a quantitative and qualitative improvement in the world and history must have taken place, and one which we can observe. Non-

Christians will deny that any such improvement can be observed which reflects credit on Christianity, while Christians are tempted to make apologetic efforts to prove that, since the cross, things have got considerably better in the world and that Christianity has proved far superior to paganism in its bountiful harvest of humanity, love and so on.

There is indeed no need to deny or minimise the fact that Christianity in practice has often shown itself superior to paganism and other national and world religions in empirically testable results. Nevertheless even a Christian who is not afraid of possible alternative assessments which could be presented on the basis of religious wars between Christians, average Christian morality, discrimination against women and so on, has really to admit that in the end the whole approach is wrong. The power of the saving will of God which is revealed in the cross of Christ as universal and finally victorious is at work and active throughout the world and not just where the cross is explicitly preached and acknowledged. In other words, in the end it is totally impossible to distinguish empirically a pure Christianity from a pure non-Christianity, and then to determine which of the two entities proves preferable to the other by humanitarian criteria. Christians are not just Christians and non-Christians are by no means just non-Christians. The most one could ask in principle is that where we find the greatest and most explicit closeness to the explicit and definitive saving event in Jesus Christ the humanitarian victory of this central saving event should be clearly tangible in comparison to the rest of history.

But how is this to be proved? Is this postulate really compelling? How does one fairly and impartially distinguish particular historical phenomena which are said to show a greater than average effect of authentic Christianity on humane values in the world from high achievements in humanity outside Christianity? How does one compare them? How does one trace them back to causes which are really in the end distinct? How can it be shown that supreme instances of humane behavior even among Christians are certainly due to a specifically Christian motivation and not other historical and social factors? To

sum up, Christians have every right, and indeed the duty, to
attribute the good they do to the saving grace of God which has
appeared to them in Jesus Christ as a definitive and victorious
promise. They may also hope that this attribution will have a
missionary effect, but they have no need to compare themselves
with those who do not feel their humane impulses to derive
explicitly from Jesus Christ. They must not misuse the grace
they have been given as an opportunity for self-righteousness,
indeed, they can and must openly and honestly recognise the
power of God's grace in the history of the human race where
they do not encounter it as explicitly Christian, and must often
accept such an encounter as a judgment on their own un-
Christianness.

The seventh enquiry forces me to say something about the
Christian doctrine of hell. The question cannot be disposed of
by embarrassed silence. In dealing with such obscure questions
one must always expect that in an attempt to answer them,
which in the end one undertakes for oneself and at one's own
risk, mentalities, prejudices and unanalysed attitudes are at
work which are the very opposite of obvious and yet are felt as
obvious. On the other hand, it is of course equally obvious that
religious doctrines of previous times grew up and were pro-
pounded under a variety of conditions which can equally be
subjected to examination.

With these preliminaries we may say that the doctrine of the
possibility that a human history of freedom may finally fail
cannot be eliminated from the Christian faith during this history of freedom. Everyone must say to himself or herself: "I
can be lost, and only through my own freedom". However,
where this freedom does not exist, or not to any meaningful
extent, there can be no question of a possibility of such a definitive failure. This failure is not a subsequent additional
punishment imposed from outside by an angry God on the real
desire of a human being for freedom, but the inner nature of
this very definitive decision of freedom. Like the correct, saved
decision of a human being's freedom, which is hidden in God,
the definitiveness of freedom's No to God cannot be envisaged
as time extended infinitely forwards; it is the eternal definitive-

ness in which freedom defines itself. *A priori,* therefore, hell cannot be envisaged as a period of time in which new events are freely possible and therefore pardon from God can eventually be expected. Freedom to be definitively against God is naturally the sheerest absurdity that can be imagined.

Those who conclude from this that such a situation, if it is possible at all, must arise only very rarely need fear no church anathema as long as they do not really seriously deny the possibility of such loss in which the punishment of freely chosen evil is identical with that evil. Such persons ought simply to ask themselves whether this is not a premature optimism which does not really take seriously the appalling horror of free evil in the world. Could it be engaging in a speculative trick or one of the exonerating techniques of modern psychology that too completely eliminates evil from the world, propelling the practitioners of viciousness and their victims into a common heaven in a rather inelegant assortment?

Where hell is concerned, we have one of the most basic examples of the state of our knowledge as creatures. A number of propositions must be maintained simultaneously, without its being possible to sacrifice one to the others and without its being possible to see clearly how they could be reconciled. There is a holy and infinitely good God. There is a just God. There is freedom among creatures which cannot be oriented to God. There is genuine freedom even in relation to this God, and therefore there is a possibility in true freedom, that can, finally, refuse assent to this God. How these propositions can be positively reconciled, are reconciled, is clearly not given to human beings to understand within the process of this freedom. But therefore to claim the right to deny one of a number of propositions when their absolute irreconcilability cannot be proved will also not do. How in practice these paradoxes (not contradictions) will really be solved we do not know.

In spite of the previous exhortations to modesty and caution with regard to an "optimism" which presented itself as too natural, there is nothing to prevent a Christian's hoping (not knowing) that in practice the final fate of every human being, as a result of the exercise of his or her freedom by the power of

God's grace, which dwarfs and also redeems all evil, will be such that hell will not in the end exist. Christians may have this hope (first for others and therefore also for themselves) if, within their histories of freedom, they seriously consider the opposite: final damnation. In having to consider this, Christians are doubtless doing something essential to Christian existence.

On the one hand no human beings may release themselves from the responsibility of freedom by pushing it off on to other causes outside themselves; on the other hand they may not regard this transferable individual responsibility as so autonomous that it cannot be seen as embraced by God's more powerful freedom and his mercy. Both of these together, though they cannot be transcended for us now in a higher synthesis, belong to Christian existence.

If we live in this sober hope, there is no need for us today to make any theoretical judgment about whether or to what extent the possibility of a human being's being finally lost really occurs. Certainly, in view of the cross of Christ, it is false and un-Christian to act as though hell was in fact the normal outcome of world history. Augustine was still able to think in that way. If it is impossible today, that is not in the end the result of our easy modern optimism; what has happened is that the consciousness of the Church has slowly become aware that in the history of a human being's freedom God in the end has the last word and that this has taken place in the cross of Christ.

To be honest, we must also admit that the emphasis in the New Testament statements on eschatology do not simply and invariably reflect what ought to be the main elements in such eschatological statements if they took their cue from the cross of Jesus, in which God's victorious mercy becomes visible and irreversible in its triumph over evil in the world. The New Testament also has a legitimate history of interpretation, as can be seen, not only in eschatology, but also in the case of many other ideas. We need have no qualms about reading the New Testament portrayal of the existence of a present or future hell as composed in the style of eschatological threatening discourses, the point of which is to illustrate the seriousness of the situation of human freedom here and now. They are not in their real content reports brought back by a visitor to the next world or the future. If these eschatological statements of the New Testament are properly read, they do not lose their seriousness and their ineradicable importance, but gain in credibility today.

Eschatological preaching today is certainly in danger of dying out; too little is said about eternity, about the way our history of freedom becomes final, or about God's judgment. But we cannot escape this danger by simply and solely repeating the old vivid eschatological threats of the scriptures or by acting (when preaching about the cross of Christ) as though it meant establishment of a mere possibility of salvation which exists as one possibility alongside the other of being damned. If this were so, then the view put forward in the seventh enquiry would be quite plausible. This says that God, in the generosity of his freedom, could always have left human beings the possibility of conversion in their freedom and so also the offer of divine forgiveness without the cross. However, if it is to be an accessible historical event that God, acting in the world as a whole, does not merely leave the possibility of repentance and forgiveness in the realm of creaturely freedom, but in fact brings about this repentance (in and through human freedom) through the power of his love, then we have precisely what the preaching of the cross and resurrection of Jesus says. This is something totally different from the pale doctrine of the two ways facing human freedom, a doctrine which seems to have been the basic pattern of Christian preaching for many centuries now. The proclamation of the cross is the preaching of God's victory over our guilt in and through our responsible freedom, not the moralistic preaching that our freedom is faced with two possibilities of which we have to choose one.

You ask sceptically, with Nietzsche, whether we really feel redeemed. Our first reply has to be to ask whether human beings today feel unredeemed, imprisoned in the hell of their guilt, walled in by their thousand finitudes and disappointments. If people today do not allow their lack of redemption to surface, but constantly find new and better ways of suppressing it with the thousands of analgesics available to them today, then they naturally cannot experience being redeemed either. Perhaps we should also analyse more precisely, more carefully, and more lovingly the triviality which disguises itself as modesty and sobriety and an admission of weakness; then perhaps in that area one might discover many Christian possibilities. But let it be. Where an ultimate basic experience of not being redeemed is not allowed to come to the surface, there can also be no experience of Christian redemption in joy and hope. However, where the experience of the prison walls of our existence is honestly and soberly admitted, where the prisoner pacing this cell no longer fearfully shrinks from bumping into the walls, there faith accepts the message that this prison has a door which has only to be pushed for an inexpressible experience of liberation.

It cannot be summoned up; it is not there to be analysed and egoistically enjoyed. But it can exist, for example as it is described in the eighth chapter of the letter to the Romans. God has managed to bring it to pass in his grace that human beings, from the depths of their freedom, entrust themselves unconditionally to God. It is the victory of the cross of Christ. When everything falls away and is abandoned in death, as it was for him, not excepting oneself, when one feels there oneself abandoned even by God because until that point God has been only the total of all that was desired and desirable or a mere pledge of that total, then God exists and appears as himself.

We have not compelled him; he has brought about through himself this ending, which is his beginning. We are free. There is an experience of being redeemed. It must grow and absorb our freedom totally. No wonder that it must be constantly sought and undergone anew, that it is constantly being covered over by the tired and sceptical triviality in which we pass our days. And yet this experience of being redeemed can constantly be enjoyed. Let no one persuade us that it does not exist. In death God's grace will have succeeded in convincing us of it, that is, of himself. Let us for the present simply have a little patience with history as it runs its course, with ourselves, and with God.

Eight

How much of what the Church says must we believe?

There is a new word in church sociology and in the language of pastoral theologians. They talk about "selective Christians"—those who identify only partially with the Catholic Church. The phrase is very apt. Men and women today are no longer prepared to accept on trust and believe uncritically what the Catholic Church presents as a truth of faith. They check, weigh things up. They accept one thing, which they regard as good and sensible, but feel no obligation at all toward another. We have already talked about the lack of appeal of the faith and here we have to say a bit more about it, this lack of appeal of the faith transmitted by the Church. What is the reason for it?

It is always a difficult undertaking to analyse the period in which one lives oneself. Today, the exact sciences seem to be losing some of their appeal. As well as the benefits of their achievements, we also see the drawbacks. The natural sciences leave human beings on their own in the crucial questions of their lives, and today we rightly refuse to elevate scientific progress as such to the status of a philosophy. Progress certainly, but not at any price! Pluralism too, the co-existence of differing world-views and beliefs, may be essential for the functioning of a democracy, but it is not an end in itself. You cannot live by tolerance on its own. You have to have convictions of your own in order to be tolerant. As a result, there really do seem to be signs of a new receptivity to the idea of a meaning for life and a goal for life—but the Catholic Church (like all the other Churches), in its present form and with its present doctrines, is certainly not in a position to give an answer to the questions of our time.

In our age, religion and life have become separated, the world of religion and the world of our everyday lives are two different realities which have become strangers to each other and think and speak in different ways. As in a marriage which has gone stale, faith and life, religion and reality, have drifted apart. Neither has much more to say to the other, and it's too much to hope for that things might be different or better. The great concepts of the faith and a thousand and one statements of traditional Christian piety no longer fit into a modern man's or woman's picture of the world, they no longer have any "life-situation". The Church's doctrinal statements fall into a void, say nothing, and so give the impression of being unusable and useless. Nor is there anywhere much sign of a new Pentecost ferment. Instead, the faith seems to be taking refuge in its own bastions. There perhaps the illusion of glory can still be maintained. So what are the reasons?

One is certainly the authoritarian appearance of the Church's official system of teaching, which is in the end simply an expression of nervousness and insecurity but has gone so far that the ordinary believer feels hardly any connection with "the people at the top". At best, statements of official Church teaching are still noted, but not really taken seriously. The theologian Walter Kasper, talking about the credibility of the Church, says: "It is no good talking in the abstract about the faith serving human freedom and at the same time operating in the Church a system of unfreedom and fear, where all the impulses of free life are monitored with suspicion and as far as possible suppressed. It is no good singing the anthem of the brotherhood of all men and continuing to maintain an absolutist régime". Many things in the Catholic Church will not do, but perhaps the most damaging is timidity, born of insecurity, which wants to preserve everything and runs the risk of losing everything. Good news? Joy? The freedom of the children of God? It would be hard to say that the documents of the

Church's teaching authority exude a spirit of freedom and joy. What do we expect from Rome except prohibitions and condemnations! You may rightly say that you too regret this, but can do nothing about it, any more than millions of "ordinary" Christians. That's one reason I don't want to keep on about this, and anyway I think that the root of the nervousness lies somewhere else. The estrangement of faith and reality has its origin in the Catholic Church's inability to express faith in Jesus Christ in the language of our time. And I really do mean language. Words like grace, mercy, reverence, loving-kindness and so on are more or less a natural part of Christian prayers, sermons and doctrines, but hardly ever appear anymore in our everyday lives. But it's mainly the mythological picture of the world in which the doctrinal statements of the Catholic faith are garbed and which makes the faith appear like a mediaeval pageant in our everyday world. The Catholic faith talks about the virgin birth, when anyone ought to know today that Mary's virginity is "only" a way of expressing Jesus' divine origin. It talks about Adam and Eve being the cause of original sin as though every child at school wasn't taught today that the Bible's picture of the world has been revised by our knowledge of evolution. It talks about the Lord's ascension and Mary's assumption, and no one can imagine what they might mean. The devil and angels are still hovering around as though the last few centuries and scientific progress had never even taken place. Is it any wonder that people are rebelling, that they simply don't believe these "fairy tales" and simply reject them out of hand?

This is only the beginning of the real difficulty. When conservative theologians refuse to touch the "demythologisation" of the gospel with a bargepole, it is certainly not because they are not prepared to admit parts of it, but because they can't see the end of a process of demythologisation (any more than in my view, the "progressive" theologians can). To give an example, there's no problem about admitting that the creation narrative in the Bible is not to be taken literally. But where do we stop? Do we have to take the resurrection literally? May we regard the existence of the devil as a bit of an outdated world-picture, but not the existence of a hell? To press the image a little further, who decides what parts of traditional doctrinal statements are the wrapper and what is the irreducible content? This is probably the real cause of the insecurity of the Church's teaching authority that we've talked about. Because people are afraid of throwing the baby out with the bathwater, they simply leave the water in the bath and that does nobody any good. It does conservatives no good because their defences are being worn away by the advance of science, and it does progressives no good because they must always wonder whether they are not giving up something which is an essential part of the faith.

Jean Améry has described the dilemma of modern theology. It can operate in the realm of mythological statements, but then the content of the statements is inevitably rejected. Or, it can make "existential" statements, but then no one knows what they are supposed to mean:

"There must be a loving Father living above the starry sky."— When an atheist or agnostic hears this he or she says, I don't believe that. I so fundamentally don't believe it that I venture to say with near certainty, "No, he doesn't live there". If someone explains to the agnostic that perhaps the greatest theologian of our time is Ernst Bloch and that God is proving his reality in history, then he or she thinks, "Yes, well, for God's sake—excuse me—perhaps yes, perhaps no, that may mean anything or nothing".

It quite often seems to me to be like that. In its effort to translate the gospel into the language of our time and to substitute our understanding of the world for a mythological one, theology comes very near to making meaningless statements. What is it supposed to mean when we are told that Christ's resurrection took place in the faith of his disciples? Should we be surprised when atheists and agnostics complain that our doctrinal statements are either mythology or simply no longer intelligible? Poetry? Literary extravagance? The reflection of attitudes or backgrounds, but not something that can be rationally challenged, because the "something" is simply no longer tangible?

So the question, "What are we supposed to believe anymore?," is quite legitimate. People today do not believe, not because they don't want to, but because they can't. They can't believe what they are asked to believe. And so they also find that the propositions of Christianity, which they know anyway, aren't much help in making sense of the world and life. Life is no easier with Christian faith. Life does not become clearer, more tolerable, more acceptable. Why does the Christian faith more often feel like a burden than a comfort and inspiration? Where it is believed, the faith is accepted much more in the sense of a "nevertheless". Some years ago J. Matthes wrote: "The contemporary interpretation of the world and life is clearly unable to integrate quite familiar knowledge about the content of the Christian religion with the basic interpretations of social and personal life". This seems to me a logical conclusion from what we have said so far.Religious knowledge on one side, actual life on the other—and the two don't meet. Life no longer receives any direction, any meaning, from religious knowledge. To appreciate the extent of the catastrophe, we need only think of the past. The Catholic of previous centuries drew from his or her faith guidelines to answer the question of the origin and the goal of his or her life. One existed to serve God, created by God. One knew where evil in the world came from and where suffering came from; one had one's place within a clearly structured society, and so on. And today?

So far in this enquiry we have been concerned mainly with the "how" of faith (which of course is connected with the "what"), but we also ought to mention the content of faith or of religious knowledge. I don't completely share the view of J. Matthes, who was quoted above. Matthes believes that: "On the whole there exists in the general population a very solid bedrock of knowledge about the Church and religion, statements about the content and meaning of the Christian faith as presented in the organised Churches". Not at all. In my view even the majority of believers do not have even a bedrock of religious knowledge. But this immediately faces me with the problem of saying what this bedrock is. Let me try and illustrate it. Imagine that you had to give religious instruction to a normally educated adult person from this part of the world. What ought such a person to know about the Catholic faith? How much can one "lose" in advance? I am not asking this question in order to get a list of the contents of the faith. I want to go back to the opening question: the problem of selective Christians. And there I ask myself: How many of the contents of the faith can one really ignore without ceasing to be a Catholic? The difficulty is clear. Either the number of believers has already shrunk to a disappearing minority, or we recognise as professing the Christian and Catholic faith even those who select, who believe one thing but not another, accept this but not something else. What do you say to a person who says that they lead a decent life, but don't need to go to mass every Sunday or to follow the papal rules about marriage? What do you say when this man or this woman explicitly claims to be a Catholic? Do you show them the door? I shall come back to this problem in my next enquiry. At the moment I simply want to express my amazement that the Catholic Church, while not tolerating the abandonment of any part of the traditional deposit of faith, knows that if these strict criteria were applied most Catholics would no longer be Catholics.

* * *

I must admit I'm a bit confused by the eighth enquiry. I can't help feeling that points are coming up again which were raised before in the first two chapters. The repetitions give one plenty to think about, and, for example, the question of the real meaning and effect of the Christian faith in ordinary life is always worth considering again. But nevertheless I would like, in the reply to the eighth enquiry, to try and discuss what seem to me to be the new issues. From this point of view, the enquiry seems to be about the ordinary average Catholic's relationship to the official teaching of the Church. This is a genuine theological question and not a purely sociological or pastoral one, and it is probably not given sufficient attention in theology. Theology must therefore be allowed a certain freedom of opinion and exploration.

Perhaps we'll get closer to an accurate understanding of the eighth enquiry if we ask first why theology has shown relatively little interest in a more nuanced answer to the question of the proper and permissible relationship of the average Catholic Christian to the official teaching of the Church. On the whole the answer given to this question has been that Catholics believe firmly and unshakeably what the Church, through its teaching authority, says is to be believed. If they fail to believe even a simple point of this teaching they are, from a theological point of view, outside the Church and heretics, at least when such a denial becomes "public", that is, even if formally they do not leave the Church.

This traditional answer to the question posed generally did not deny, though it also did not make very clear, that this answer about the obligation to believe and the choice in faith, strictly speaking, applies only to actually binding dogma and not to other teachings of the Church's teaching authority. Indeed, this limiting clause is even today not very clear to the average Christian, and also applicable only to a very limited extent, because it is far from easy, and in specific cases even the theologians find it hard to decide what, apart from the most obvious basic substance of the Christian faith, is binding dogma. Official statements in papal encyclicals and so on even more or less deliberately leave the distinction between "ultimately binding" dogma and "not ultimately binding though authentic" teachings of the Church unclear, and prefer to stress that an ordinary Christian has a duty to accept even official teachings which are not in the strict sense dogma. On such a reductionist interpretation, we could say straightaway that the eighth enquiry is quite right when it says that the great majority of actual Catholics are not Catholics without qualification, but ought to be regarded as selective Christians.

The cultural explanation for the reductionist attitude is simply the mentality of earlier times. In those former ages the average individual, unless he or she rebelled as the result of his

or her own thinking, genuinely and positively believed the prevailing opinion in society, what the intellectual and social élite,
the rulers of the state, regarded as true and proper. In a society
in which attitudes were so homogeneous, in which a few set the
tone for all, opposition to society's generally accepted beliefs
(especially when it was to be expressed publicly) took a great
deal of thought and trouble. In the same way the reductionist
interpretation presupposed that in matters of religion persons
reach their convictions by a considered and firm assent of their
reason and freedom. (In a remarkable show of optimism, it
used to be held that even religiously uneducated and primitive
people held rationally based beliefs about their particular religious tenets, and even quite natural "doubts" about truths of
faith were regarded as a denial of them.)

This general attitude to matters of faith derived from the
particular general attitude of a period which has now passed or
is rapidly disappearing. It was taken for granted that the totality of a person's fundamental convictions were based on absolute conscientious decisions made in freedom. These cultural
hypotheses can no longer be accepted. This is why the question
of the actual and permissible relationship of an individual's
attitude in fundamental questions to the official teaching of the
Church requires a more nuanced answer. If such an answer
can be given at all, it can only be given piecemeal. "Is" and
"ought" must always be distinguished, though at the same time
always connected.

First we must take an unprejudiced look at the new basic
structure of attitudes in modern men and women and allow it
its due weight. The old general answer took it for granted that
the attitudes of a person which are important for his or her
authentic, religious existence, are composed of fixed and unconditionally accepted basic religious convictions. These were
supposed to be maintained clearly and unshakeably, even
though the phenomenon of a change in such fundamental
convictions, conversion and so on, was naturally not totally ig-
nored. Naturally we do not want to deny that free moral existence is inconceivable without some sort of basic axioms, even if
the basic axioms were merely the conviction that such basic

axioms do not and cannot exist. The belief that selfless love and egoism are not equally valid bases on which to build one's life, that it is wrong to exploit another human being for one's own advantage and so on, are today existential basic axioms of this sort and, even when we infringe them, they retain an absolute claim on our assent.

Nevertheless, even if such fundamental absolute norms are still valid today, there are two differences from the past. In the past these fundamental axioms were specific and were regarded as simply identical with the fundamental dogmas of Christianity, identical in that both were taken as premises: There is a God, the ultimate guarantor of the moral order, there is a judgment, there is an eternal life, there is forgiveness promised to us through Jesus Christ who was crucified and rose from the dead. Even if we are quite sure of the existence and fundamental importance of certain fundamental axioms of behaviour, not even we Christians can any longer simply maintain that these axioms are in practice identical with the fundamental dogmas of Christianity.

Identical in practice here means identical in terms of our immediate response. I do not, of course, deny that as a matter of fact they are ultimately identical, that, for example, an absolute moral demand can and in the end must be shown to be a demand of "God". Nevertheless, it will require long and patient work by Christianity to show this. The second difference between our present attitude to ultimate questions and that of previous ages is the fact that our modern attitudes, without prejudice to the existence of the fundamental axioms we have mentioned, largely consist of opinions. We need these for our own existence and yet are unable to give absolute assent to them. We regard them, on the one hand, as unavoidable, and yet cannot allow that they are more than probable, provisionally valid, may become outdated and have to be replaced.

The people of earlier periods lived, as far as religion and morality was concerned, in a dimension in which there were only truth and error. Today we live in the dimension of what is provisionally probable and more probable, questionable and fundamentally always open to revision. This is valid simply as a description of an intellectual climate, and applies to Christians as well, particularly when, as citizens of an increasingly mobile world, they have as their neighbours representatives of all religions and must accept that they have just as much intelligence and integrity as Christians. In addition, this "softer" outlook, because it is felt to be constantly developing and changing, is made up of a much greater variety of individual elements (individual facts and motivations) than in the past, which the individual is no longer in a position to draw into a definite synthesis. The outlook of our world differs from that of previous periods in being made up of provisional and conditional opinions, which it is no longer possible to combine totally into a fixed "system".

These are the basic factors which must be taken into account in any answer to the new general question of the possible and proper relationship of the individual today to the official teaching of the Church. First of all it is understandable and proper for the Church as a whole, in its official representatives, to identify for itself the basic axioms by which it lives and works with its basic dogmas. It could indeed be shown that even in the official understanding of the faith a certain distinction is made and is legitimate between these two things. Examples of this can be observed in the teaching of the Second Vatican Council. Nevertheless, the number of distinctions possible is hardly even hinted at. The official Church starts from the existence of God, from the existence of his revelation in Christianity. It proclaims these and the other fundamental dogmas of Christianity as essential, and leaves Christian apologists with the wearisome and often unsuccessful task of showing the credibility of these basic Christian dogmas a second time in terms of fundamental theology (notably with reference to the existential basic axioms which men and women of our time accept as valid for themselves).

This position of the official Church is understandable and backed by a tradition of almost two thousand years. Even so, it might be asked whether the Church's official preaching of Christianity ought not seriously and explicitly to accept as Christian the basic axioms men and women of today find immediately and definitely credible. This might be the only way not only to present existing Christian dogma as credible, but also to reformulate it so that the appeal from this dogma to the basic axioms which are immediately accepted today has real force. Whether, if such a process did slowly take place and were successful, we should once again have a simpler and more obvious identification between the official formulations of the Church's teaching and generally accepted contemporary basic convictions, or whether a degree of separation between the two is inherent in human intellectual history, remains a question which for the moment has no answer.

But what is the individual supposed to do about his or her "faith" in relation to the official teaching of the Church? First, it is natural that the individual's "faith" should not simply be in its content the reproduction and repetition of the faith of the official Church. Just as the intellectual, scientific, and cultural consciousness of a people at a particular time is not simply present as a whole, in its fulness and complexity, in the mind of an individual person of that period, while the person is nevertheless a full member of that people and its intellectual history, it is not the case that the only Christian faithful to the Church is the one who keeps in his or her head, in a more or less complete and organised form, all the doctrines to be found in Denzinger!

A normal Christian, who cannot be asked to engage in lengthy theological studies, may quite properly, in relation to the Church's general consciousness of its faith, make emphases and select. This is quite possible without requiring a positive rejection of what is left to one side in such a selection. Naturally such a "selection" and individual reduction must be coherent, and normally the selection and structuring of the individual's awareness of faith are naturally for the most part the unnoticed result of his or her particular situation, though to some extent it is also quite legitimately the result of conscious decisions, in which a person takes an interest in one thing and ignores something else.

Today Christians in their situations certainly have the duty and the right, when making such a selection, to concentrate on the most fundamental issues of the Christian faith and to leave much else to one side because they cannot yet fit it in. Christians, in committing themselves to faith, should know why they believe in God, should have the courage to appeal in prayer to this mystery of their existence, and to hope for eternal life. They should look to Jesus, who was crucified and rose again, and derive hope from him that all the fatal absurdities of their existence and their sin will be dissolved in the light and love of God. They should have the will to belong, in a sober religious "socialism", to the company of those who have the same faith and the same hope and who are trying to love one another.

But supposing that a Christian does this, does he or she not, for example, need to find out more about what is really meant by "original sin", what precisely is meant by the immaculate conception of the blessed Virgin and so forth, whether and why there are just seven sacraments, what the hypostatic union in this Jesus of Nazareth means, what the infallibility of the pope means and what it does not mean? No one is banned from finding out more about such matters. But when this is not possible, or one fails, or a person simply ignores such matters, he or she is still a good faithful Catholic.

We cannot say that everything expressly mentioned in an official church catechism is part of the basic substance of the Christian faith. All honour to the person that knows all that. In many cases, however, it would be even better if a person knew less but in his or her life acted on it in a clearer and more radical way. The person whose faith involves such a "selection" is not a selective Christian, but a quite normal member of the Church. This is really a truism automatically practised quite happily by countless Christians. However, there are today more complicated people, intellectuals, who think they can be members of the Church honestly only if they consciously know at least the contents of a medium-sized catechism in detail and have actively made it their own by existentially appropriating it. But then they find the pressure too great and think they cannot honestly be Christians in the Church.

Christians who select in this way, but are not selective Christians, are not at all denying what in their own spiritual economy they leave to one side. Only a really firm denial, with the whole weight of the freedom which decides on life and death, would destroy an individual believer's positive relationship to the consciousness of faith of the Church as a whole, and, if the denial were made in public, would deprive such a person of membership in the Church. In the case we are discussing, however, there is no such explicit and firm denial. In such a case a person of our time in particular must allow the outlook we were discussing above to operate. Outside the religious sphere, too, people today are familiar with a whole range of different views and opinions out of which they find it, in their particular situations, impossible to make a positive, clear and absolute choice of one. They remain undecided and let things ride. This is possible in our case too; the co-existence of opinions covers a greater area than firm judgments.

There is also another reason why it applies in our case. A Christian in a particular case in which he suspends final judgment between two opposing views is usually not at all sure whether his understanding of a theological doctrine of the Church that seems to be in contradiction with another of his views in fact really reflects the Church's teaching and is also really in conflict with this other view. In the actual case he or she will probably not be able to find a way out of this situation of uncertainty, and therefore has the right to leave the whole problem alone.

It could be objected that a Catholic Christian is only really a Catholic Christian if he or she formally assents, with an absolute assent of faith, to the infallibility of the Church in its teaching (under the familiar conditions). In other words, the Catholic can and must in the situation described say: Because of the formal authority of the Church I accept a particular doctrine of the Church even though I cannot see it as true in itself or cannot myself trace its theological derivation from scripture and tradition, and I therefore, because of the formal authority of the magisterium, firmly reject an opposite doctrine. In other words, it could be said that the suspension of judgment in more complicated cases which are not of vital significance for the ordinary religious life of a normal Christian is not allowed for a Catholic Christian because his or her assent of faith to the formal authority of the Church's teaching office does not allow him or her to persist in such a suspension of judgment.

In reply to this objection we may say that, in terms both of the objective importance of the articles of faith and their inter-relation (the hierarchy of truths), and in terms of the practical reality of life, the formal authority of the teaching office (in the absolute Catholic sense) is not at all the most fundamental truth, nor the one which is most easily arrived at subjectively. On the contrary, despite its formal importance for the whole of Christian teaching, it is a relatively secondary and far from accessible doctrine. We believe (in principle and in practice) in God, in eternal life, in Jesus Christ and so on and *therefore* in the Church and its formal teaching authority, and not the other way around, even though these more fundamental truths in practice (historically and through education) come to us from the Church.

But this is by no means to say that a first encounter with the Church is itself an acceptance of its infallible teaching author-ity. It is the other way around: in the ideal case the religious awareness, of God and so on, which the Church mediates may in the end lead (logically and psychologically) also to an ac-ceptance in faith of its absolute teaching authority. Augustine's remark that he would not believe in the Gospel unless the Church's authority made him, is wrong, however pious and obedient it may sound. Logically and existentially, in other words, belief in the authority of the Church is one of many truths which we arrive at, if at all, and only in a slow process of discovering the faith. What we have found, inevitably found, about many other articles of faith also applies to this one, even if this article in itself has a retroactive formal significance for our knowledge of other aspects of faith.

In fact, of course, in the life of the Church nobody is ever pursued as a heretic for not explicitly professing the infallibility of the Church's teaching authority as an absolute religious con-viction, provided only that he or she does not firmly and pub-licly deny it. This practice of the Church is not simply justified by the practical impossibility of any other course in such a large religious body, but has a fundamental theological justification. A finite human being is always quite properly some way behind the absolute universality of the whole truth; he or she can only bear it when he or she does not have to bear its whole weight. If it is true that an ordinary Christian's subjective catechism does not have to be positively identical with even the penny catechism (desirable as this might be), it might indeed be appropriate for the official teaching of the Church to consider more closely what it is required to proclaim to the people of our time with spirit and fire as the alpha and omega, and what it could afford to say more casually and perhaps even less precisely.

This conception of a looser relation on the part of the individual Christian to the teaching of the official Church does not lead out of the Church nor does it place us on the fringes. It does not in any way mean that the elaborate and complex teaching of the Church as it has developed in the historical process stretching over several hundred years has no importance or is at most a byproduct of an intellectual game played by theologians or even by the rabbis among them. The great and developed truth of Christianity in the general consciousness of the human race through all times and places honours God, the eternal truth. And in different places and periods clarifications of specific theological questions may be essential for particular people and groups in the Church.

At this point the question naturally arises (and it is of great importance for an ecumenical theology) whether the Church can and may later "forget" truths which at a particular historical moment it had to express in great detail. In the year 2000 will a Latin American or an African Christian, a preacher of the gospel, a theologian, legitimately feel a remote connection, shrunk almost to historical curiosity, with the Council of Trent's scholastic teaching on justification, similar to that which we feel today with the Council of Orange? Even defined truths of faith are part of a history which is not yet finished and which is also the further history of these same dogmas. It is also always possible that doctrinal definitions which seemed almost to have disappeared from the world of our real concerns may suddenly reacquire a totally new importance and power, and theologians, where they work seriously, can make us aware, nor just negatively, but also positively, of the significance of old dogmas.

So far we have tried to sort out our ideas about the relation of the individual "normal Christian" to the defined substance of the faith. We have not discussed the question of distinguishing between dogma and other authentic teachings of the teaching authority and cannot discuss that further here. However, we must say something about the relation of the individual Christian to teachings which the teaching authority of the Church puts forward and defends without claiming for them the force of dogma. Pius XII's rejection of polygenism and Paul VI's teaching in *Humanae vitae* are just two examples from the recent past. In most cases these will be doctrines which ordinary Christians can simply take or leave because they don't affect them very much. Nevertheless, as the two cases mentioned show, there are authentic teachings of the official teaching authority for which the rules of practice stated so far are inadequate on their own. In such cases we may say what the German Bishops' Conference said in a declaration before *Humanae vitae* and later applied to *Humanae vitae* in the so-called Königstein declaration:

With regard to an error or a possible error in nondefined doctrinal statements of the Church, which may themselves possess a number of different levels of authority, it must first be recognised soberly and calmly that human life quite generally must always be based, "to the best of one's knowledge and in all good faith", on knowledge which cannot be regarded theoretically as absolutely certain but which, "here and now", because at present it cannot be improved, must be respected as a valid norm of thought and action. Everyone knows this from his or her own life, every doctor in a diagnosis, every statesman in his judgment of a political situation and the decision he bases on this judgment is familiar with this fact. The Church too, in its teaching and practice, cannot always and in every case accept the dilemma of either making an absolutely binding doctrinal decision or simply being silent and leaving everything to the arbitrary opinion of the individual. Anyone who thinks he or she has a right to a private opinion, or already knows what the Church will eventually decide to be right, must ask himself or herself, in a sober self-critical assessment before God and conscience, whether he or she has the necessary breadth and depth of specialised theological knowledge to deviate in private theory and practice from the current teaching of the Church's teaching authority. Such a case is conceivable in principle, though subjective arrogance and a hasty assumption of being in the right will have to be answered for before God's judgment.

An earlier passage in the statement dealing with nondefined teaching of the Church's magisterium said explicitly:

> We [the Bishops] mean the fact that errors can affect the Church's teaching authority in the exercise of its office and have affected it. The Church has always known that this is possible, has said so in its theology and has developed rules of practice for such a situation.

As we said before, these authentic, non-defined doctrinal decisions, which are liable to error, are not always simply theological subtleties of no interest to a normal Christian. The resistance of the official church to the liberal and democratic movements in bourgeois society in the nineteenth century, which were not just matters of practice but also official teaching, the reactionary condemnation of many opinions of modern exegesis, much in the wholesale condemnation of modernist opinions at the beginning of the twentieth century, the condemnation of the "pill" by Paul VI, these and similar declarations by the Church's teaching authority which are open to challenge also concern lay people in the Church. In this respect the stress on the specialist knowledge of theologians in the sentences just quoted from the German Bishops' Conference needs to be qualified, because in some circumstances it places the ordinary Christian in too much of a position of inferiority. In general, however, theologians give considerable scope to the individual sense of truth, and, for an ordinary Christian, a life and death conflict with the Church over its teaching authority would really only arise in connection with the fundamental substance of the Christian faith.

Of course, because of the nature of the discussion in this chapter, the positive function for the normal Christian of the official teaching of the faith has been too little emphasised. But of course it does exist. Even Christians who, because of their education and their contacts with non-Christian culture, feel severe tensions between their individual consciousness and the official proclamation of the faith, should be clearly aware that they owe the basic substance of the Christian faith by which they live to the Church, its authority and its institutions.

Much of the tension in the relationship between the individual and the Church's authority and institutions derives not so much from the teaching of the Church, as from its practice: the way it treats the individual in its actions, its law, its ordinary community life and so on. But no doubt we shall have occasion to talk about this when answering a later enquiry.

Nine

In the Church

For some time now there has been a "third denomination" among the Christian Churches, a Christianity professed and practised by people who, while feeling no particular obligation toward the doctrines and moral rules of the established denominations, nevertheless want to be Christians. These people are dismissed by the pillars of the Church, by committed members of the Church, as nominal Christians or "Sunday Christians". The pastoral theologian N. Mette remarks about this, however: "These and similar labels are not really the result of a theological judgment. They tend instead to belong to the sphere of social psychology: they are used as a defence against a tendency within the Church felt as a threat, in other words for reassurance".

I am surprised that the Church's teaching authority has not yet found the right attitude to these Christians and that there is still no official statement. Are they afraid? Are people afraid of a break, before a sober admission that the strictly Christian Churches have long ceased to be comprehensive? There is an awareness of the problem at meetings of Christian academics and in the publications of pastoral theologians.

It is no accident that the subject is often discussed here under the heading "Youth without rules?", because the areas of friction between the Church and the younger generation have been shown statistically to be not so much the dogmatic propositions of the faith, but the rules of conduct laid down by the Church. In short, people no longer live in the way the Church demands and prescribes. This is true most of all concerning the reception of the sacraments and of marital and sexual morality. H. Weber has summed up the situation neatly: "The actual situation is, to put it briefly, that the structure of rules preserved in the Church and still preached in it is largely being abandoned." If we remember that this abandonment cannot be possible in the long term without serious sin and a loss of the (sanctifying) grace of God—at least that is the teaching of the Church—and that this is by no means a failure as a result of momentary weakness but a fundamental attitude (which no one thinks of confessing!), then the Church's attitude is surprising. Ought not the Church to make a stand? Ought it not to say—with the corresponding actions—that with a basic attitude of this sort it is impossible to be a Christian? In other words, shouldn't we just tell the "long-range Christians" that their Christianity is not recognised and that they are excluded from the Church? Today that would be all the easier since even the Catholic Church, since the Second Vatican Council no longer links salvation exclusively to sociological membership in the Church, but promises salvation also to those who live by their conscience, even outside the Church. Of course, a theologian of the traditional mould might say there was no need for an explicit excommunication of "fringe Christians". He would say that by living in serious sin they are automatically no longer true members of the Church. But, frankly, I would call that cheating. And there's another thing we should do. We should refuse to baptise the children of these ex-Christians, refuse to marry them in church, refuse them a Catholic burial and—last but not least—do without their offerings. But of course it doesn't happen.

I am not trying to imply that it's the money which decides. Quite the opposite. I think that the official Church, without admitting it, has slipped down from its high horse, and simply doesn't dare to say openly what it tolerates. What is it precisely?

People today can no longer see that official Church pronouncements about ordinary life are more than merely one opinion among many, an opinion which has to prove itself in practice and shows its value in real life. Here practice has long ago overtaken theory. Theoretically, the "simple faithful" know nothing of the subtle distinctions theologians make between the statements of the magisterium. But the "simple faithful" know that the Church's rules are not the gospel, that they have been affected by all sorts of factors, have been subject to various historical influences and so on. So they select. They accept the rules which help them to cope with their lives and leave those which seem to be simply arbitrary.

And there is another point. In the age of pluralism, in a period in which people live by different catechisms, we can see for the first time that there are other ways of doing things, perhaps better ways. This puts a question mark beside our own norms and commandments. We ask what their point is, and in the end that seems to be the main argument. Rules that people don't see the point of they don't keep. I start from the position that the Church's regulations, rules and commandments do not exist to force us into self-denial, but in the long term are meant to be for our benefit. On the other hand, when I am told that I must do this or that and not do one thing or another, I am not satisfied simply to be told it's the will of God, which the Church claims to know. I also have to see that doing or not doing a thing is of benefit to my life, that living in this way is good. That is precisely what is so often missing. The Church can no longer put its values across. It cannot say (and, in contrast to the past, today it has to do this) why this or that is compulsory and something else is forbidden. This creates the impression that the official Church is the real successor to the pharisees and scribes against whose legalistic religion Jesus protested so vigorously. It lays burdens upon people which it is not prepared to bear itself. But what are the specific issues?

First I want to mention something that's not an issue. Wherever the Catholic Church—as it has always done and continues to do—works for a just solution of social problems such as the situation of the developing countries, the equality of men and women of different races, basic human rights, works of charity and much more, it may be sure of the support of all its members. And even in individuals' private lives when particular events in life such as birth, communion, marriage and funerals have to be specially marked and celebrated. I don't think that the action of the priest and the Church here is just to organise the celebration or the festivity. In this area people today still have genuine religious needs and expectations. The Church is needed in this area. But where are the problems?

First there is that broad area of everything connected with sexuality and marriage. I don't know. Are people today, especially the "younger generation" so often mentioned in this context, all lechers who just cannot restrain their sexual desires, and engage in activity which is harmful to them and harmful to the human race? Surely word must have got around that even in our time rules and structures are accepted which are certainly felt to be enriching because they stress partnership and honesty in relationships. What is the real justification for the rule that sexual relations should take place only in a legitimate marriage? Certainly not all the ideas going around today on this matter are right, but don't we allow the people of today any feel for what is possible or right? Particularly when social and—it is no exaggeration—biological conditions have changed, when we have proper contraception. How can we defend the rule that a marriage performed in a Church must be kept in being at all cost, even if the happiness of the partners and that of the children is damaged by it? How can we justify the rule that a termination of pregnancy is always forbidden when anyone can always imagine situations in which a woman is physically and emotionally destroyed? It may sound hard and unfair, but it's hard to avoid the suggestion that it is the hang-ups of the single and the celibate's "revenge" which can only accept all or nothing. Isn't it in fact the so-called "fringe Christians" who are beginning to show that the Christian faith can be lived in ordinary life without the often hypocritical and dishonest attitudes of an outdated marital morality and marital laws? Just in passing, we might mention that people today find it very hard to understand—for all the possible theological and sacramental distinctions—that a priest can marry relatively easily in spite of his promise of life-long celibacy, whereas a marriage may never be ended. The clergy, people feel, are always able to find a loophole where there are none for the simple faithful.

People today also reject what might, with a slight over-simplification, be called a "sacramental routine". Of course, this includes a number of Christians who keep away from the Church more out of convenience than as a result of a lack of understanding. For the majority, however, it is probably true that they don't see the point of regular confession and attendance at Sunday mass—and whose fault is that? The "Church" says so—that's not good enough anymore. In sermons and religious instruction the Church has an opportunity to explain the meaning and necessity of the reception of the sacraments. It can't do it. It fails. I refuse to believe that Catholics don't want to receive the sacraments because they don't understand them. It is understanding that is missing, not good will and readiness. So the churches get emptier and emptier. Parishes are no longer living cells of the community but only entities tossed together by the accidents of district boundaries, and, moreover, the laity still have no voice. The "Church" is still the clergy when it really comes to decisions. Can you imagine an official statement on sexual morality being produced in the Catholic Church by doctors and psychologists?

One can think of so many things. I am not inclined to give up easily. I don't want to sacrifice the faith to an un-Christian fashion. Being a Christian will always mean going against the tide, carrying the cross. But the crosses in life are heavy enough already. They don't need to be multiplied and made heavier by the commandments of the Church. Everyone probably sometimes has the feeling of being at a turning point in history. All the same, it seems to me, with all due caution, that the Church is going to have to decide and find a way forward. It will have to free itself from the dead weight and dust of history, for the sake of the gospel. A new reformation cutting right across the denominations! Sometimes I think that's just what we need. And I sometimes wonder whether it isn't these very "fringe Christians" who are the heralds of a new way of belonging to the Church, the "third denomination", those who have already separated the essentials of the faith from the inessentials and are living only by what they can honestly live by. I wish the Church had more confidence in its own future. I wish that the

Church, and all Christians, would start to make sure again that the fire doesn't go out, but keeps burning.

Applied directly to this ninth and last enquiry, this would mean that I wish that the teachers and preachers of the Catholic faith would ask themselves honestly what norms, commandments and regulations they have to lay down for the salvation of the human race. Not because it's always been that way, but because they themselves do not want to stand before God's judgment seat if they have not promoted salvation. They should ask themselves honestly what commandments and rules of conduct they are not completely convinced about. Which, in their own view, are not crucial to the salvation or damnation of human beings. One of the things we will be judged by is having imposed unnecessary burdens on people. Will the faith one day be once more what it ought to be, good news?

*   *   *

I can't help feeling that the ninth enquiry is the most difficult of all. Practical living is more difficult than all the abstract theories which rightly "abstract" from much and so make the problem simpler. Another problem is that in answering this question it is impossible to leave out certain general topics connected with membership of the Church, while it is also impossible to say nothing about particular topics such as sexual morality and so on, even if comprehensive discussion of these particular topics cannot be expected here. We can only discuss them insofar as they affect the relationship of an individual Christian to the Church.

It may seem complicated, and may provoke all sorts of questions, but it is nevertheless true that the relationship of the individual person and Christian to the Church (in terms of "identification" and/or "distance") can be very complex and can therefore also take on very different forms. Some factors affecting this relationship are easily identified, for example, being baptised or not being baptised, and perhaps also the presence or absence of outwardly visible religious practice. However, the realities which constitute the relationship of a Christian to the Church also include others which are not so easy to identify,

which change more easily and which even the person concerned finds it far from easy to pin down. All the more, then,
will this be the case for the society in which the person lives.
Belief, moral attitude, inner personal commitment to the life of
the Church, are all such realities which play a role in a person's
membership in the Church, but are hard to identify. Another
difficulty is that in the history of an individual life they change,
obviously or unnoticed, are perhaps not sufficiently thought
about, and coexist in the most remarkable ways, not only with
the easily identifiable elements of a relationship with the
Church but also with all the other elements which make up a
person (character, education, history, environment, and so on).
We may confidently say that every person has his or her own
unique relationship to the Church.

If we think about this, it should not be a criticism of the
official Church that, if not always clearly and consistently, at
least generally it is generous and tolerant in making distinctions between those it regards and treats as its members and
those whom it classifies as no longer or not yet its members.
Given the great number of elements which affect a relationship
to the Church, it would be theologically and speculatively possible to make the most diverse explicit distinctions. And very
different distinctions have been made in the course of history.
Today the Church's practice tends towards recognising as
members of the Church all those who have been baptised, have
grown up in some connection with its ministry and have not
explicitly dissociated themselves from it by a legal declaration.
(Of course I realise that all this is very vague.)

The point is that in the making of these practical pastoral
distinctions the individual's subjective faith and subjective
morality is not taken into account, simply because it is hard to
identify and also in constant change. The Church feels that in
its pastoral mission it is under a particular obligation to all the
baptised and refuses to cancel this special obligation unilater-
ally. It does not regard itself as a select club of the particularly
orthodox or holy. The Church's often apparently illogical in-
clusion in this way of many baptised people when they themselves seem to place little value on membership in the Church is

easier to understand if in the case of rejection of the Church we distinguish between a merely "objective" situation and a responsible decision, a decision which the Church too has to make. This is the problem for ecclesiology. Such a rejection of the Church, while in one sense, "objectively", a separation from the Church, in the theological sense may, on the other hand, for the person concerned not be an existentially significant decision and so involve no serious guilt. It is difficult to say whether and how far such a rejection really separates a person from the Church, particularly when it has no clear public embodiment. In this light it is understandable that the Church makes a formal declaration of separation, or officially ratifies a separation which has taken place, only in very rare cases.

Let us look at the whole problem not so much from the point of view of the Church, but from that of the "individual fringe Christian". I tend to think that even today average Christians or average persons do not easily get into such a serious conflict with the Church in the strict theological sense that they inevitably feel separated from the Church from their own point of view or from that of the Church. Even today many more people could have a genuinely positive, happy relationship with the Church than in fact do.

As far as the theological and doctrinal side of this problem is concerned, the most important points have already been made in the answers to the previous enquiry. A Christian today has no illusions about being personally infallible; he or she holds views for which he or she has a certain preference with a degree of sceptical reserve and ultimately suspends judgment. In such a case if the relevant opinion seems impossible or difficult to reconcile with the teaching of the Church, although the person firmly holds the basic Christian substance of the faith, tries to keep it alive and develop it, and in this has a sense of being in grateful harmony with the faith of the Church, then he or she is in the faith of the Church. It does not matter that for the moment a positive and general harmonisation of the official teaching of the Church in its full scope and much else that is in the person's consciousness is impossible.

The same applies to the "morality" of a Christian, both in its theoretical formulation and in its practical application. The principles worked out in the answer to the last enquiry for the relationship between the official doctrinal teaching of the Church and individual views naturally apply also to the moral teaching of the Church and the individual's attitude to that.

With regard to the moral teaching promulgated and defended by the official church, it must first be realised that the area of what is proclaimed as dogma by the ordinary or extraordinary magisterium probably scarcely goes beyond what the moral sense of a normal person even today, especially in our part of the world, regards as strictly binding. In other words, apart from possible theoretical exceptions, which we cannot go into here in further detail, differences between the official moral teaching of the Church, which it rightly proclaims in accordance with its duty, and the conscientious moral judgment of the average person today on more serious issues will by and large be differences associated with an authentic teaching of the magisterium, but not with an actual dogma of moral teaching. In such a case there exists the leeway mentioned in the answer to the previous enquiry. For example, when a doctor in an extreme case finds a medical justification for a termination of pregnancy and performs an abortion, and feels in conscience that his action is not only legitimate, but in fact an obligation (all of which is quite conceivable), then, while he or she may be going against the traditional teaching of the authentic magisterium, which rejects a direct termination of pregnancy for any reason whatever, he or she has nevertheless not gone against the dogma of the Church and may be able to cite not only subjective reasons in support of his or her action ("invincible error"), but possibly objective arguments. A doctor in such a situation may believe that he or she is objectively right and that the contrary teaching of the Church is too black and white and needs revision, and may well be revised as moral theory develops, because in principle it has always been recognised as reformable or could have been so recognised. The doctor, therefore, need not regard his or her real relationship to the Church as disturbed by such a course of action.

There can be many other such cases, for example in the area

of sexual morality. While there is no room here for a detailed discussion, it may be said that by no means all that is taught, defended, and insisted on in practice by the Church's teaching authority is the absolutely binding teaching of the Church in such a way that to contravene it would in itself constitute a breach with the Church.

Today in particular, because of the constantly increasing speed with which internal and external factors of human life are being separated, partial conflicts between the moral teaching of the official Church and the individual's subjective conscience may easily arise, but these should not be given too much importance and not be regarded as absolute. The individual has no right to avoid a serious conscientious decision and a really self-critical consideration and examination of his or her moral judgments, as the German Bishops' statement quoted above insists. Nevertheless theoretical and subsequent practical deviations from an authentic teaching of the Church are conceivable in the area of morality as in other areas and need not, when viewed in correct perspective, necessarily and always make a Christian a fringe Christian with a merely "partial identification". Of course the position is complicated still more by the fact that conflicts may arise between an individual Christian and the institution of the Church when the Church (rightly or wrongly) is convinced of the correctness of the rules of conduct it promulgates and acts accordingly within its domain. It refuses a Church marriage even in a case where an individual is convinced of the nullity of a previous marriage but cannot prove this to the Church's authorities. In its own hospitals it does not tolerate a doctor who terminates a pregnancy even in an extreme case. It places obstacles in the way of a theological career sometimes even in cases in which it cannot be maintained that the reasons lay in clear contraventions of certain dogma, and so on. Such conflicts are conceivable, happen and cannot be removed merely by general principles and an honest desire for mutual understanding and tolerance. At least not all of them can. It would be wrong to eliminate such insoluble conflicts by a theory in which the Church never had the right to act according to beliefs which even it regarded as merely authentic and not infallible. Certainly the number of such conflicts for which there seems to be no solution could be kept lower than it seems to be. Let us stress once more the true position. There are many Christians who regard themselves, because of their beliefs or their way of life, as on the fringe of the Church, although by real theological principles they are by no means on the fringe; they are within the area of diversity in identification with the official Church in its overall teaching and actual practice which is legitimate for a completely faithful member of the Church.

All our comments on this question so far have been very general, so we shall now attempt a few more specific remarks on individual problems.

First there is the issue of sexual morality, in which a serious and painful discrepancy exists or seems to exist between the officially promulgated teaching and the rules accepted as valid in this area in present-day society. In this whole area a great many things are obscure and uncertain, without much hope that these obscurities will very soon be removed. We have already said that it is not certain that each and every specific rule put forward in this area by the Church has absolute validity now and through all periods of human and social change, at least in the form in which it is promulgated by the Church.

One reason why this is not certain is that even this official teaching of the Church on sexual morality can be seen to have undergone very considerable changes in the course of history, and much that was previously rejected as immoral or as more or less sinful today no longer attracts the Church's disapproval. This is not to say that the genuine fundamental substance of the Church's teaching on sexual morality does not exist in the calm and assured doctrinal consciousness of the Church, or continue to be firmly held and to constitute a binding norm for Christians in the Church. Nevertheless there are a great number of specific problems in this area for which the solutions offered are not simply guaranteed by the infallible magisterium of the Church, but represent an authentic but reformable teaching and therefore do not remove all the theoretical or practical difficulties.

For example, one may have not the slightest sympathy in theory or practice for homosexuality and yet wonder whether it is absolutely certain that any conceivable form of homosexuality in any person is an objectively serious contravention of human nature and dignity. It is not so totally certain that the New Testament simply forbids, in every conceivable case, divorce followed by the remarriage of the divorced party; it is not even quite clear precisely what the Church at the Council of Trent really defined about the indissolubility of marriage. To a certain extent it is even unclear how far general changes in society's consciousness take place not merely in practice in the area of morality (something no one can doubt), but also help to form that particular "nature" from which, according to the traditional teaching of the Church, the moral norms of the "natural law" are derived.

This would mean that the natural law itself, while not changeable in a simple sense, nevertheless has a history of its own, a view which of course cannot be seriously disputed. This is therefore another reason for the large area of obscurity in sexual morality. This needs to be seen more clearly and also recognised more honestly in the Church's teaching, not as an easy way around the hardness of the internal law of human nature, but as a way of appealing to individual moral responsibility and choice, which can never be replaced by any official Church casuistry. This would make it possible to avoid or reduce much of the irritation in the Church which arises from conflicts between an official sexual morality presented with little understanding and the moral sense by which people today actually live.

There is also a lot of obscurity about moral norms for sexuality before marriage. It does not promote human maturity if all sexuality before marriage is more or less tabooed as it used to be and treated as nonexistent. It is equally foolish and unrealistic to trivialise pre-marital sexuality and reduce it to pure physiology. But what course is to be taken in practice between these extremes, the normal teaching of the Church doesn't seem to be very sure. But is it really a bad thing to admit this and to tell individuals that this is another area in which the

Church has no patent remedies which are absolutely sure and have only to be followed—as far as possible—literally? The "adult Christian" does not require the Church to provide such simple formulas, but nevertheless takes its teaching seriously and knows that human sexuality must exist in the context of true love and reverence for the human being as a totality, and stands under the will and judgment of God.

We must also say something about "sacramental routine", as the question describes it. There is no space here to discuss the meaning of sacraments in general. If human beings are bodily and social creatures and if their relationships with God also cannot suddenly exist in spiritualistic interiority alone without dying, there is no cause to doubt the fundamental justification and meaning of sacraments. For ordinary Catholic Christians this means first of all that they have their children baptised. In this connection we may note briefly that there are other cases in human life in which an existentially significant gap in time exists between a call and an answer and that it is therefore not surprising that a certain separation in time should exist between God's promise to a human being in infant baptism and the acceptance of this promise by that person in faith, hope and love. Indeed, such a separation cannot be avoided, because it is only throughout his or her whole life that a person can or must accept the promise which God made to him or her in baptism.

For the Catholic Christian the "sacramental routine" also means the so-called "Sunday obligation" and the obligation of annual confession. This immediately raises the theological question which has not yet really been fully discussed, whether the so-called "commandments of the Church" are only the expression (perhaps in a specific application) of a religious demand on a Christian's conscience which is inherent in the nature of Christian reality, or whether in this case we have a commandment of the Church as such, which, in that specific function, no longer coincides immediately or exactly with sacramental reality. Let us assume that the first alternative is correct, while remembering that the freedom of the children of God may no longer be limited, as it was in the Old Testament, by ritualistic commandments. It is nonetheless obvious that a

Catholic Christian has an obligation to celebrate the death and resurrection of Jesus in the liturgy frequently because these are the basis of his or her salvation in life and death and, if the eucharist really was instituted by Jesus, a Christian cannot be indifferent to it and at the same time claim that the cross of Christ is the fundamental basis of his or her salvation.

Once this is accepted, however, a measure of generosity in the interpretation and observance of the Sunday obligation is quite legitimate. A Catholic Christian should certainly try to shape his or her own religious development in such a way that frequent participation in the celebration of the eucharist, in other words, in practice at least on Sundays, becomes a need and a natural part of his or her religious life, but there is no need to regard the formal fulfilment of a commandment of the Church every Sunday as a matter of life and death. If a person holds the theological view that the second of the two alternatives presented above is correct, and is an essential instrument in the fight against a regrettably widespread indifference to the Sunday celebration of the eucharist, he or she must find his or her own way of supplementing the Church's Sunday obligation with interpretations and qualifications which will prevent this commandment from becoming part of a legalistic sacramental routine.

No one who does not take a magical view of the sacraments can deny that one genuinely religious participation in the memorial of the death of Jesus means more than two fulfilments of the "Sunday obligation", which would amount to little more than being present twice in a Church building. (Naturally a genuine religious participation in such a liturgical event is not guaranteed by the fact that it takes place only once and not twice.) Routine can be harmful, and one genuine and responsible way of attempting to counter this (though not the only one) may be for a person not to venture too often into the neighbourhood of this enormous event of the death of Jesus and so to ensure that participation in the eucharist does not become a pious routine.

As regards annual confession as a commandment of the Church, the first thing which has to be said honestly and clearly is that in any interpretation which is valid today, and at least since the time of Thomas Aquinas, the commandment of auricular confession is only binding when objective and subjective contraventions of God's absolute will exist which are so serious as to bring a person into radical contradiction with God and make him or her liable to eternal damnation unless genuine repentance arises from the centre of his or her existence. Apart from this case, an "auricular confession" may not only be possible as a sacrament, but also of the greatest human and Christian value, but it is not a commandment of the Church in the strict sense. Participation in a "service of penance" may sometimes be a better way of achieving peace of conscience than a routine private confession.

Of course it remains a question whether we should imagine that in a normally serious human and Christian life such "serious sins" constantly occur within a single year, making annual confession for the general run of Christians a real obligation and not just desirable. On this question there is no single view among Christians, among psychologists of religion and specialists in religious education or among theologians, and also no really binding declarations of the magisterium. It could be held that the more pessimistic view of the life of the normal Christian was sanctioned by the practice of centuries down to our own time according to which all Christians did confess at least once a year, and also legitimated by the normal practice of religious instruction which usually passed over the clause about the existence of really severe sin at least in silence when stating the obligation of annual confession. But this is no proof of this pessimistic interpretation of the average Christian life. And anyone today who hears the good news of the victorious grace of God and the divine mercy and knows a little about modern psychology will find it hard to believe that a normal human life is constantly swinging between an absolute existential Yes and No to God.

The modern theologian will also point out that traditional moral theology even quite recently has described as objectively seriously sinful acts of which no sensible person today would dare to say this. The extraordinarily large decline in frequent confession and even in "Easter confessions" may be very regrettable from many points of view, but it is hard to prove that the majority of the cases which fall into this category in fact represent a contravention of a strict commandment of God or of the Church.

We have gone into all this here only to make clear how much discretion a normal Christian in the Church enjoys if he or she feels threatened or restricted by a sacramental routine in the Church. Objectively no such threat or restriction really exists. The scope for the individual to shape his or her own religious life is much greater than most Catholics think. It ought to be used. Not in petty haggling about what is "obligatory" in the Church and what is not (or no longer) but in a genuinely creative initiative to develop one's own religious life, claiming Christian freedom boldly without feeling that more is demanded of one officially than one can really honestly and genuinely do.

Some serious reader of this answer may have got the impression that this is another timid and ultimately cowardly surrender to a moral laxity which seems to be gaining the upper hand in the Church. Such a reader should first reflect that Christianity started with the slogan that the Christians were those who did not want and did not have to carry the burdens which were laid on their fathers even though they were unable to carry them. Such a reader should also feel a responsibility for ensuring that the Church is not presented as the human race's bad conscience and that the holy will of God proclaimed and defended in the Church should not be felt as a burden and a restriction, but as a vitalising force rising from the deepest core of human existence.

God takes responsibility for his world and is more powerful than evil (otherwise he could never have permitted it) and such a reader should try to let God's optimism overcome his or her own pessimism and look out into the world and learn to feel that world history, despite all the terrible lapses and all the evil, is moving relentlessly toward God. And the reader should then look at the Church. The Church (how could it be otherwise?) reproduces in itself the world with all its sin, with its limitations and stupidities, with the inevitable problems of any institution, with the constant antagonism between the permanent and the changing, and so on. We should really have to leave the world if we were to leave the Church because its pettiness and sinfulness above and below us was too much for us. However, we would thereby lose what remains the distinguishing mark of this Church.

The Church, in professing and bearing witness to Jesus Christ who was crucified and rose from the dead, is always the witness to the eternal hope. And it is better to hope, to hope absolutely and without limit, to hope against one's own hopelessness, than to despair. No one has seriously dared to claim that in order to be able to hope in this unlimited and absolute way it is necessary to make an absolute decision against Jesus who was crucified and rose from the dead and because of him in the future to make an absolute decision against his Church. Many people have found that it is possible to have this hope of infinite life within the Church. It may sometimes seem that in the Church we very often have to appeal to the essence of the Church in protest against its embodiment as a way of improving its embodiment, but why shouldn't something of the sort be part of a Christian's task?

Nevertheless even this, like so much else, is secondary in comparison with the one task common to all in the Church: waiting for eternal life. Our earthly life now seems to us, despite all the brevity, which we also feel, very long and filled with an endless variety of tasks, possibilities, defeats and triumphs, which we call world history and our own lives, and this immeasurable range of possibilities and tasks must be taken seriously because in it and only in it do we reach eternity. Nevertheless, in the end the whole of this world history and our own history is only the inexpressibly short, lightning moment between the empty void and God, in which God succeeds in creating freedom for others and in giving himself to it.

"I believe in Jesus Christ"

Here, at the end of this little book, we want to try to sum up what we have been saying. This is independent of particular questions, which have drawn our attention more or less at random in particular directions and to particular problems. Another reason why such a summary seems appropriate is that not only did the questions represent a not entirely obvious selection, but the very answers to these questions were, for a great variety of reasons, a rather arbitrary selection. Of course, since it is not our intention merely to reproduce the teaching of the Church's magisterium in the words and traditional style of the magisterium, but to try to say what we think we have heard and understood in hearing this official message, even such an attempt at a balanced summary remains to some extent subjective. It leaves the reader with the question whether and how he or she can transfer what we have written into his or her own intellectual framework and to some extent reconcile it with the rest of his or her experience.

The remarks which now follow are not written from a "neutral" point of view, but from a "committed" one, that is by a person who hopes that he is a Christian as well as he can manage. This naturally entails a degree of subjectivity, which there is no way of excluding or bypassing. We know that these pages are the product of the fact that I have been a Christian all my life and have practised theology for almost sixty years. I know that in these pages I am defending my own existence. I can even ask myself whether, when I write these pages, I am presenting with sufficient clarity and honesty all the problems and experiences which have naturally constantly threatened and modified a lifetime's belief in my own case. On the other hand, awareness of such an ineradicable subjectivity does not destroy the right or possibility of writing this because the ultimate issues of life can be expressed in no other way. Since they are all-inclusive, there is no position outside them from which they can be assessed and justified. Where the opposite assumption is made (for example in neutral religious studies), either the object of the enquiry has already been misunderstood or it must be admitted that the real object, the question of life and death where a final Yes or No is demanded, is simply not being dealt with. The personal approach (which does not mean the subjective, because by its very nature it is committed to a maximum of objectivity) is here the only approach which beings us close to objectivity.

I shall, therefore, try to report what I am trying to say and be when I say: "I would like to be a Christian". One has to say here, "I would like to be". In the Christian view, one must in the end leave it to God to decide whether one really is—in theory and, above all, in practice—what one claims to be and automatically is in social life and in the Church on the surface of everyday life.

I would like to be a person who is free and can hope, who understands and shows by his actions that he himself is at the mercy of his freedom, a freedom which throughout life is creating itself and making him finally what he should be according to his original pattern of human nature, a person who is faithful, who loves, who is responsible. I am well aware that such words can very easily sound very lofty and theoretical, that they create a feeling that real life is being shrouded in a haze of fine words, but also that in their meaning they are far from "clear". We can ignore the first difficulty because no one, not even the most primitive materialist, can do without ideals which, because they have not yet been reached, draw one on and keep one's life moving. As to the second difficulty, the vagueness of the "ideals" just mentioned, this must be admitted. All words which express or invoke the totality of human existence are "unclear": that is, they cannot be defined by being assigned a place in an intrinsically clear system of coordinates distinct from them. They are "unclear" because they point to the one, most real, absolutely single totality which we call "God". For us, however, this "unclarity" has an absolutely positive and irreplaceable function, and a person who does not accept this "unclarity" as a good and a promise drifts into trivial stupidity.

I am convinced that such a free history of real self-determination takes place in and through all the impenetrable details, and uncertainties, perplexities, inadequacies, all the starts that never reach a tangible goal, and all the internal and external determinisms which fill our lives and make them, even for ourselves, almost a meaningless accident. I am convinced that a human being's historical life moves in freedom toward a point of decision, that it contains this decision in itself, that life as a whole must be answered for and does not simply run away into a void in these details. Of course, this outlook on which my life is based, which is almost inescapable and yet required of me, is nothing but breathtaking optimism, so terrifying that everything in me trembles with the sheer audacity of it.

Yet I cannot give up this attitude, cannot let it decay into the triviality of the everyday or the cowardice of scepticism. Of course philosophers and other theorists of human life can talk forever about the meaning of freedom, responsibility, love, selflessness, and so forth. Nor do I find such terms clear and transparent. Nevertheless they have a meaning and guide choices in the thousand and one trivia of life. It may seem that such words can be analysed psychoanalytically, biologically and sociologically and revealed as an avoidable or unavoidable superstructure on much more primitive things, which alone can count as true reality. I also constantly discover cases in which, to my consolation or my horror, such detailed analyses are in fact correct. And yet because in such attempts at analysis as elsewhere it is always the same responsible subject which is at work, and is responsible even for this destruction of its own subjectivity because it is the subjectivity that does the work, in the end, on the whole, such attempts at destruction are in my view false.

I am not trying to escape from myself and have no desire to escape from my responsible freedom as a true subject. Will this being left to oneself end in my case in a final protest or a final acceptance? Since I exist and an acceptance is so firmly planted in me and my freedom, my acceptance seems to me in one sense so obvious an implication of the ground of reality that I often feel that all protests against one's own existence in its full particularity are no more than passing incidents in a fundamentally universal acceptance of oneself and the whole of one's existence. On the other hand I cannot escape the knowledge that a subject's freedom cannot be directed simply to this or that particularity alone, but existence as such, and that therefore the temptation to straightforward rejection, to a total protest (which is the essence of true sin), always exists and can become a reality in the triviality of a banal existence.

I accept myself. I accept myself without protest with all the accidents of my biological and historical existence, even though I have the right and duty to change and improve those elements in it which I feel oppressive. It is this very critical desire to change my existence in all its dimensions which is the form and the proof of the fact that in the end I really accept this existence. But for all the hope of really changing something, this existence (my own and that of others, for which I also feel responsible) remains opaque, burdensome, will not dissolve into controllable transparency; it remains short and full of pains and problems, subject to death, to which all generations remain exposed.

I accept this existence, accept it in hope. I accept it in the one hope which includes and supports everything, which one can never know that one really has (or only pretends to have because at a particular moment one feels marvellous). This hope, whose inner light is its only justification, is the hope that the incomprehensibility of existence (for all the obvious beauty it also contains) will one day be revealed in its ultimate meaning and will be this finally and blissfully. It is a total hope, which I cannot replace with a vague mixture of a little hope and unadmitted despair, though this may always also be present in the deepest core of existence when the foreground of my life seems to be occupied by nothing but meaninglessness and despair. This all-embracing and unconditional hope is what I want to have. I declare my allegiance to it; it is my supreme possibility and what I must answer for as my real task in life. Who will convince me that this is utopia, that such a hope is false and cowardly, worse than if I let myself fall into a radical scepticism which is theoretically possible, but in the reality of life where we take responsibility and love is impossible to maintain? This ultimate basic trust in the complete and comprehensive meaning of existence is not a free-floating ideology; it not only supports everything else, but is also supported by all the other experiences of life. It includes (at least partial) experience of meaning, light, joy, love and faithfulness, which make an absolute claim.

These specific experiences which support ultimate hope just as they are supported by it will have to be discussed later. For the present, I take it for granted that we are above the dull naiveté which thinks (as even sophisticated scientists sometimes do) that matter is more real than mind or spirit, which floats over matter as no more than a sort of exhalation or side effect of physical constructions. These "materialists" do not see that they cannot come into contact with this matter except through mind, or they are totally unable to say what matter as such really and fundamentally is.

This free fundamental act of existence, which can only be described haltingly and of course does not exist only where it is explicitly talked about, moves towards what or, better, the person, we call God. I know that this word is obscure, by definition the most obscure word there can be, the word which it is genuinely impossible to include among the other words of human language as one more word. I know that what is meant by the word may be present in a person's life even if its name is never spoken by the person. (Anonymous theists do exist because in the totality of reality God is not a particular entity like Australia or a blackbird, which one really doesn't need to know anything about, but supports everything, is the origin of everything, permeates everything and therefore exists and rules anonymously but genuinely as the unexpressed condition of possibility for all knowledge and all freedom wherever mind is at work.) I know that today what we mean by God is very difficult to imagine by means of the image of a great architect of the world (which was still acceptable in the period of the Enlightenment). I know that the word "God" has been used to do any number of terrible and stupid things. I know that it is very easy to keep on finding, in oneself and in others, stupid misunderstandings which do their mischief under cover of the word "God". And yet I say that the ultimate basis of my hope in the act of unconditional acceptance of the meaningfulness of my existence is promised to me by God. This does not make him the projection of my hope into a void for in the instant that I envisage God as my projection, "God" becomes meaningless and ineffective for me. Equally, I can no more abandon the basis of my hope than abandon the hope or identify it with my powerless, finite self, which has to hope, no more make myself God than I can simply think of this God as outside me and one thing alongside others. God must be what is most real and what embraces all things in its support for him to be at once the basis and goal of the unbounded and unconditional hope which becomes a basic acceptance in trust of existence.

On the other hand, this God is incomprehensible mystery. This hope (in which reason and freedom are still united) transcends any possible explanation because every detail which can be understood and included as an element in the equation of life is and always remains influenced and threatened by others which have not been included. Even in everyday life we experience the unboundedness of our transcendence of what is nevertheless not subject to our transcendence.

In addition, human transcendence in knowledge and freedom also shows this. It can neither be made to stop at a particular point nor derive power from any "nothingness" (because "nothing" can do nothing), and moves towards mystery as such inasmuch as by its own power it is completely unable to fill the infinite sphere of consciousness. But the miracle of existence is not so much that there is this mystery (who can really deny it except by obstinately refusing to take an interest in it?), but that we can and may become involved with it without being tossed back in that very instant into our own nothingness (to the point where atheism becomes the only form of recognition worthy of God).

The act of accepting existence in trust and hope is therefore, if it does not misinterpret itself, the act of letting oneself sink trustfully into the incomprehensible mystery. Therefore my Christianity, if it is not to misinterpret itself, is my letting myself sink into the incomprehensible mystery. It is therefore anything but an "explanation" of the world and my existence, much more an instruction not to regard any experience, any understanding (however good and illuminating they may be) as final, as intelligible in themselves.

Even less than other people do Christians have "final" answers, which they can endorse with a "solves everything" label. Christians cannot include their God as a specific understood element in the equations of their lives, but only accept him as the incomprehensible mystery, in silence and adoration, as the beginning and end of their hope and so as their only ultimate and universal salvation.

The movement of finite mind towards God in such a way that God becomes the content and the goal of this movement and not just the initiator of a movement which in the end remains far from him in the finite must be supported by God himself. Because Christians know that this fundamental trust of theirs, because it is really absolute and desires God himself, is supported by God himself, they call this most intimate movement of their existence towards God by the power of God "grace", "the Holy Spirit", and express this single movement towards the immediate presence of God in faith, hope and love.

Christians believe that anyone who is faithful to the dictates of his or her conscience is following this intimate movement in God towards God. They believe that this movement takes place even if a person does not recognise it for what it is, and has been unable to see its historical manifestation in Jesus Christ, even in the descriptions of an explicitly Christian faith. Christians fear in their own case (and therefore in the case of others) that in the final balance of their lives they may freely say No to this deepest movement of their existence in an open or concealed unbelief or lack of hope. However, at the same time they hope for all others and so also for themselves that this movement may find its way through all the darkness and superficiality of life to its final "eternal" goal. Christians accept this ultimate threat to themselves from themselves (to freedom from freedom, which can say no to God). They keep on overcoming it in the hope that the human race's history of freedom, which is in turn contained by the freedom of the incomprehensible mystery and by the power of his love, will on balance have a happy outcome through God. It makes no difference to this that no theoretical statements can be made about the salvation of individuals—in other words, that in the present absolute hope is the ultimate.

All that has been said so far forms for me, as a Christian, a mysterious synthesis with the encounter with Jesus of Nazareth. In this synthesis primal hope and knowledge of Jesus form a circle which is in the end unbreakable and give each other mutual support and justification before the intellectual conscience of a person who wants to be honest—but with an intellectual honesty which includes what we Christians call "humility". Through the mediation of the message of Christianity and the Church in the gospel of Jesus, and also supported by that ultimate hope in grace, the Christian encounters Jesus. The experience of this synthesis between ultimate primal trust in grace and the encounter with Jesus is naturally somewhat different in the lives of different people, and there is a difference in particular between those who throughout their conscious lives have been Christians and those whose explicit encounter with Jesus for their salvation took place only at a later stage in their lives. However, since the grace which moves all human beings is the grace of Jesus Christ even if the person who receives grace is not consciously aware of this, and since all love of neighbour is, by Jesus' own statement, love for him even if a person is not consciously aware of it, this synthesis (at least as an offer made to freedom) is present in every human being. As far as this synthesis is concerned, therefore, the distinction between Christians and non-Christians (a distinction the importance of which should be neither underestimated nor over-

estimated) relates, not to its presence, but to its conscious realisation in explicit faith. So in this synthesis who does a Christian
recognise Jesus as?

This experience in which Jesus becomes for a particular person the event of the unique and qualitatively unsurpassable
and irreversible approach of God, is always affected by the
totality of its elements as a single entity even if each of the
elements is not necessarily immediately present explicitly and
clearly in conscious awareness. There is Jesus, a human being
who loves, who is faithful unto death, in whom all of human
existence, life, speech and action, is open to the mystery which
he calls his Father and to which he surrenders in confidence
even when all is lost. For him the immeasurable dark abyss of
his life is the Father's protecting hand. And so he holds fast to
love for human beings and also to his one hope even when
everything seems to be being destroyed in death, when it no
longer seems possible to love God and human beings. But in
Jesus all this was supported and crowned by the conviction that
with him, his word and his person the "kingdom of God" was
made finally and irreversibly present. Christians believe that in
Jesus God himself was triumphantly promising himself directly
in love and forgiveness to human beings. In Jesus God, on his
own initiative, was bringing about and also proclaiming his
victory in the human history of freedom, and so of course
creating a new and ultimate radical situation of choice for the
person who hears this message.

In Christianity this experience of Jesus includes the assur-
ance that this is a man in whom reality does not lag behind the
demands of human nature, despite the scepticism produced by
the rest of our experience of human beings we can here really
rely on a human being. This does not mean that we have to
have a stylised picture of Jesus as a superman. He had his
limitations, even in his teaching and its presentation, because
this is an inevitable part of being a real human being. But he
was the person he was supposed to be, in life and in death. His
disciples, who witnessed his downfall on Good Friday without
illusions, discovered in themselves, as something given by him,
a certainty that life was not destroyed, that death in reality was

his victory, that he was taken into the protection of the mystery of God, that he "rose". Resurrection here of course does not mean a return into our spatic-temporal and biological reality, but the definitive rescue of the whole human being ("in body and soul") in God. Because this resurrection is being accepted by the mystery which, in its incomprehensibility, is called God, how it happened is impossible to imagine. However, where our absolute hope and the experience of this life and death meet we can no longer think in terms of Jesus' destruction without also denying our own absolute hope, without, whether we admit it or not, allowing ourselves to fall in despair into bottomless emptiness and ultimate nullity.

When, in our own hope for ourselves, we try to find somewhere in the history of the human race a person of whom we can dare to believe that here the hope that embraces all the dimensions of our existence is fulfilled and that this fulfilment itself makes itself known to us, that is, appears in history, this search can find no identifiable figure without the apostolic witness to Jesus. In the first place at least, amazing as it may seem, we simply can find no one who, according to the testimony of their disciples, made this claim. (If we also accept this claim as the guarantee of our own salvation, it then becomes even more unusual.) If, through the witness of the apostles, we have experienced the risen Christ, that experience gives us then the power and the courage to say from the centre of our own existence, "He is risen." The fundamental structure of human hope and its historical experience form a unity: he is the one who has been accepted by God. The question which human beings constitute for the limitlessness of incomprehensibility has been answered by God in Jesus.

Here human existence has finally achieved happiness in the victory achieved from both sides, the victory of grace and of freedom. Here the sceptical doubts about human beings in their uselessness and sin have been left behind. Jesus regarded himself in life and word as the irrevocable coming of God's kingdom, God's victory in human freedom achieved by the power of God, and his self-understanding, which derived from the unbreakable unity of his unconditional solidarity with God and with the world, is confirmed by what we call his resurrection. He is now both the question and the answer present in human life. He is the ultimate answer which cannot be bettered, because every other conceivable question for human beings is made superfluous by death and in him this all-consuming question has been answered if he is the risen one and irrevocably promises us the incomprehensible boundlessness of God himself, alongside which there is nothing else which could be question or answer. He is the word of God to us, the answer to the one question which we ourselves are, a question no longer about a particular detail, but the universal question, about God.

From this position, the statements of traditional ecclesiology and theology about Jesus Christ can be recapitulated and at the same time protected against misunderstandings. We can say what is meant by his "metaphysical divine sonship", by the hypostatic union of the eternal word of God, by the complete and unimpaired human reality in Jesus, by the communication of idioms. This Christology, which is more than fifteen hundred years old and even today for the most part shared by all the main Christian Churches, is still valid and will continue to be so, because it expresses, remorselessly and correctly, what the Christian faith experiences in Jesus, God's irrevocable promise of himself to the world, which is historically accessible in its irrevocability.

On the other hand, it is possible for these official Christological formulas of the Christian Churches to be misunderstood and then rightly rejected. They do not simply need repeating to be immediately understood; and the orthodox believer, while he may explain them, may still admit that what they say can also be said in other ways. Anyone who says in the orthodox sense that Jesus is God has stated the Christian truth, provided that he correctly understands this statement, which cannot be taken for granted. This also implies the converse, that anyone who accepts Jesus as the insurpassable word of God to himself or herself, as the final confirmation of their own hope, is a Christian even if he or she cannot reproduce, or can reproduce only with difficulty, these traditional Christological formulas, which derive from a conceptual framework which it is hard for us to recover.

The cross and the resurrection belong together in any authentic faith in Jesus. The cross means the no longer obscured requirement that human beings must surrender completely before the mystery of existence, which human beings can no longer bring under their control because they are finite and sinful. The resurrection means the content of the absolute hope that in this surrender there takes place the forgiving and blissful and final acceptance of a human being by this mystery, that when we let go completely we do not fall. The cross and resurrection of Jesus together mean that precisely this letting go without falling took place in an exemplary way through God's act in Jesus and that we too are irrevocably promised this possibility (including that of being able to let go, which is the most difficult task of our lives) in Jesus.

Here, in Jesus, we have the "absolutely particular". We need only to rely on this particular person lovingly and absolutely. (In the end the interposition of time is no more an obstacle to this than that of a body. We only have to take a chance.) Then we have everything. True, we have to die together with him, but no one can escape this fate. We should not try to squeeze past death until others—emphatically not ourselves—can no longer notice whether we accept our own death. So why not die with Jesus, saying in unison with him, "My God, why have you abandoned me?" and, "Into your hands I commend my spirit"?

Only here does all the metaphysics about human beings become real. And it is no longer so important what the metaphysics is or might be like "in itself". By the time it has arrived at Jesus, it contains very little, and therefore everything. Because it treats reaching death as reaching life, and there we have the answer to the question, all or nothing! Not in talking about death, but in death, his and ours. Not until this moment, which for oneself is still to come, has one finally embraced Christianity.

Nevertheless, even beforehand we can prepare to be open to this event. This training for dying does not destroy the splendour of the life we lead now. Let those who can and want to

enjoy this glorious life. But let them enjoy it with an eye on
death. Only in death does everything acquire its ultimate importance and so become the "light burden". Christianity is for
me the simplest way because it embodies the single totality
of existence, plunges this totality calmly and hopefully with
the dying Jesus into God's incomprehensibility and leaves all
the details of life to us as they are, but without giving us a
formula.

Nevertheless the simplest is also the most difficult. It is grace,
the grace offered to all, which can be accepted and (this is
Christian hope) is accepted, even where absolute hope has still
not explicitly found the person it is looking for as its embodiment, Jesus of Nazareth. Perhaps it is ordained that many
"find" him more easily by looking for him in anonymous hope
without being able to call him by his historical name. If the
conscious personal history of the human race forms a unity,
everything in it is important for all and for that reason the
original sacrament which is Jesus Christ has been established
from the beginning above all the periods and spaces of this one
history, but over it as over a history in which necessarily not
everything can be at the same historical distance from everything else or have the same explicit closeness. Nevertheless,
anyone who has met Jesus with sufficient clarity must acknowl-
edge him because otherwise he or she would be denying his or
her own hope.

If the resurrection of Jesus is mystery victoriously promising
itself to us by the power of God as the mystery of our definitive
life, it is certain and understandable that his resurrection
would not exist if Jesus did not also rise in the belief in his
eternal validity. It is for that reason that there exists the community of people who believe in him as the one who was
crucified and rose from the dead. This community is called a
Church all the more because those who believe in Jesus Christ,
simply because of their shared reference to the one Jesus just
cannot simply be religious individualists. Nor can this faith in
Jesus be transmitted without active witness, which again ultimately requires a social structure in the community of faith
which gathers round Jesus.

For this and many other reasons Christianity means Church. Human beings are social beings always driven even by the history of their ultimate freedom from a socially constituted community and toward one. Even the most radical religious individualist is still related to the Church by language, holy scripture, tradition, and so on even if he or she wants to make himself or herself totally independent of it. Truth, too, is connected with an open and yet critical relationship to society and therefore to institutions, though this does not mean that an individual's "own" truth can be something arbitrary. Truth which is not constantly seeking to communicate itself to others in unity and love, and which is not constantly given to the individual by a community, is not truth, because in religion truth is the consciousness of the person who gives himself or herself to others in love.

Nor can this truth in community escape the solidity inherent in the social nature of a community. The various Christian Churches and denominations may not attach exactly the same value to the Church, but throughout Christianity there are institutions, and therefore in principle there is a desire for the Church. Where individual freedom and uniqueness (which are essential to a Christian) exist as the individual's immediate relation to God, and yet because of them religious groups and a Church are necessary, there will always be the permanent tension, which constantly takes different forms and must always be resolved afresh, between Christian freedom and the Christian need for the Church. This tension cannot be resolved either by an ecclesiastical totalitarianism (a genuine danger easily underestimated by ecclesiastics) or by a Christian anarchism, nor can there ever be such specific rules for dealing with it in particular cases that a solution could be merely an administrative matter of applying the rules. In the end it is only in hope that the individual Christian can endure this tension in patience, in the hope that one day the eternal kingdom of love will exist and not the Church. Nevertheless the recognition more or less everywhere in the Christian world of baptism as the rite of initiation into the Christian community in the confession of the divine Trinity is a universal admission in principle that membership in the Church is an essential feature of Christianity.

I do not want to say much here about what in the Christian world is the bitter topic of the divisions between the Christian Churches, this problem which has produced the most terrible events in Christian history, religious wars between Christians. Today this question, which has existed throughout almost the whole history of Christianity, exists perhaps primarily as the question whether and in what way the Christian religious conscience has to make a distinction of religious significance between the different Christian denominations and churches. In the past the question did not take this form. Hitherto (and quite properly, on their terms) all the Christian denominations were convinced that the diversity of creeds and the ecclesial institutions which held them were not simply purely accidental and ultimately unimportant variations of the one Christian faith, but that they raised a genuine religious question for the conscience of each individual. It was held that true Christianity, which alone led to salvation, was to be found only in one or other of the denominations and Churches. Today, whether we like it or not, the situation in this respect has certainly become more difficult for the average Christian. On many issues at least, it is no longer so easy to say whether the various Christian creeds are really in direct contradiction or whether they are all (or many of them) simply expressions of the same single Christian truth and reality within different conceptual frameworks and with different linguistic resources and different, historically conditioned, emphases, and would therefore certainly all find a place in the one Church.

Christians throughout the world have come to realise that the diversity of church laws, rights, customs and spiritualities can be much greater than that which European Christendom was previously used to. It has at least become clear in principle that one Church does not mean the same canon law in all its detail. The historical accidents, which in themselves have nothing to do with the unity of faith and the unity of the Church and yet have played a very important part in the division, are well known.

Everywhere there is a growing understanding of the need

for ecumenism. In such a situation it is certainly no longer so easy to regard one of the Christian confessions and Churches, to the exclusion of all the others, as the only legitimate one and the only route to salvation. There has of course been progress in this difficult situation, even where (as in the Roman Catholic Church) there is not yet a willingness to recognise all the Churches with their different creeds and institutions as in principle equal in status. The title "Church" is given on all sides, the universal validity of baptism is stressed, there is a recognition of the genuine religious value of many doctrines, institutions, and form of spirituality in the various churches, rejoicing at the identity of holy scripture throughout the Christian world, and so on. However, these very attempts at ecumenical rapprochement have made it much more difficult in practice, at least for Catholic Christians, to still allow their Church the unique status which, even at the Second Vatican Council, it claimed for itself as opposed to all the other Christian Churches.

Today there are also all the difficulties of historical knowledge which affect the precise connection between even the most primitive stage of the Church and the historical Jesus and also the impossibility (at least for the average Christian) of deciding rationally which developments in subsequent church history are legitimate and which illegitimate (or at least not binding in faith)—and there certainly have been both. In this situation even Catholic Christians have to distinguish between the content and absoluteness of their assent in faith to their Church, if they can give such assent, which is in principle possible and required, and the arguments from fundamental theology which justify this assent but are in themselves external to it. The two are not the same, as every traditional fundamental theology knows. The true assent of faith accepts the actual Church as it understands itself.

On the other hand, as regards fundamental theology and the external justification for this assent, the average Catholic will answer yes to a double question and thus legitimise his or her relationship in faith to the Roman Catholic Church. A Catholic will ask whether he or she can find in this Church the liberating spirit of Jesus, his truth, without at the same time encountering obstacles in the shape of the Church itself or its doctrine or an absolutely binding practice. A Catholic will ask whether he or she, despite and through all historical and unavoidable change, can find in this Church the clearest and strongest possible connection in historical continuity with the beginnings of the Church and so with Jesus.

An affirmative answer to this double question seems to me, a born Catholic, to give me the right and duty to maintain an unqualified relationship with my Church, a relationship which naturally, by its nature, includes a critical attitude to it as the locus of evangelical freedom. How a non-Catholic can come to the Catholic Church, something which is in principle possible, is a different question and one which cannot be explored further here.

Every true Christian naturally suffers because of the social and historical structure of the Church. In its empirical reality the Church always lags behind its essence. It proclaims a message by which its own empirical reality is always called in question. The Church is also always the Church of sinners, whose members by their actions deny what they profess. In fact the Church cannot in this connection rely totally on the argument that it is made up of human beings and therefore, like every other historical community or association, reveals human nature. The Church's role is to be *par excellence* the place in which the power of grace demonstrates its victory over the depths of malice and narrowness in human beings.

Of course the Church can point to people in whom this power of grace is really made manifest, but are such people that much easier to see in the Church than outside it? How is one expected to prove that without becoming pharisaical and arrogant when one really honestly looks "outside" the Church for such people? A difficult question. Quite enough terrible and base things have happened in the history of the Church. There is so much that is terrible and base that the only helpful answer is this: where else would we go if we left the Church? Would we then be more faithful to the liberating spirit of Jesus if, egotistical sinners that we are, we distanced ourselves as the "pure" from this poor Church? We can do our part to remove its meanness only if we help to bear the burden of this wretchedness (for which all of us too bear some guilt), if we try to live in the Church as Christians, if we help to bear the responsibility of constantly changing it from inside. The Church in all denominations must always be the Church of the "reformation".

If we believe we can discover some element of genuine Christianity in ourselves and understand what it really means, how then can we refuse to graft it unselfishly into this community of sinners? Are they not in fact, through the power of the spirit of Jesus, moving through all the wretchedness of history towards that fulfilment promised by the death and resurrection of Jesus to all of us and not just to a small élite among the human race?

Christians have always known, in theory at least, that they can only know, make real and credible their relationship of hope and love to the incomprehensible mystery of their lives in unconditional love for their neighbour, which is the only way we can really break out of the hell of our egotism. This love for others in all the varied forms which it can take is by no means so straightforward, even without being distorted into a method of covert egotism; it is the liberating grace of God. Where this love is real, the spirit of Jesus is at work, even if it is not named, as Matthew 25 clearly teaches us. We can only say in trembling: Let us hope that the grace of God is working this miracle somewhere in ourselves! Everything depends on this, absolutely everything.

Of course in a period such as ours it has to be realised that this love of neighbour cannot possibly be itself if it lends grace and dignity merely to the private relations of individuals. Today it must also be practised particularly (though not only) as the responsibility of every person and every Christian for the social domain as such. It must take the form of justice and peace because in the end justice cannot be sought by a compromise of merely rational calculation, but only by the occurrence often enough in society and history of the absurd miracle of selfless love.

And the other way around, this miracle is concealed in sober calculations of justice. Social and political responsibilities have a particular form for the individual Christian, individual Christian groups and the Church as such. The Church must make its love of neighbour credible through its commitment to action in society and against it. There is a horrifying amount of injustice, violence, alienation and war in the world and all this injustice adopts the disguise of inevitability, cold reason and legitimate interest. Because sinful Christians in a sinful Church are beneficiaries of this injustice, whether they know and admit it or not, the critical function of the Church is society cannot have as its true and own responsibility the defence of a socio-political status quo. If it gives the average person the impression that it is a support of a conservative system, if it wants to be on good terms with everyone instead of, like Jesus, preferring the poor and rootless, if it receives more sympathy from the socially secure and the rich than from the poor and from the oppressed, then there is something wrong with this Church.

The Church must carry out its critical commitment in society under the guidance of the spirit which has been given to it, the spirit of Jesus, and in the hope of eternal life. The memory of the death and resurrection of Jesus gives the Church a critical distance from society which allows it not to treat as absolute (explicitly or covertly) either the future already achieved or the nearest feasible future. If the Church were to develop into a merely "humanitarian concern" it would be betraying its responsibility because its task is to proclaim to human beings the ultimate seriousness and incomprehensible dignity of this love for human beings. But even today the greater danger seems to be that love of neighbour, and our neighbours today are mainly secular society, is not taken sufficiently seriously by Christians. And yet this is the only place where the God whom the Christians are looking for can be found, with Jesus, not even he dissolved the incomprehensible mystery, but accepted it in faith and love by refusing to make a choice between love of God and love of human beings.

Christianity and the Churches are slowly acquiring new and much more complex relationships with the non-Christian world religions than they had in the past, when these religions were outside the cultural orbit of Christianity. Christianity cannot withdraw the claim to have heard and to preach the universal and unrepeatable word of grace in Jesus, who was crucified and rose from the dead. But Christianity does not for that reason deny that the Spirit of God is carrying out its liberating work throughout history in the middle of human limitations and culpable confusion, the Spirit in whom Jesus surrendered himself to God in death.

The non-Christian world religions also bear witness in their own way to this spirit and not merely to human limitations. Many of their provisional and important experiences may be included as elements of an answer in the all-embracing answer which is Jesus because the history of the Christian message is by no means yet at an end. Nor can Christianity treat atheism, which today has become a mass-phenomenon on a world scale, simply as a manifestation of rejection on the part of human beings who refuse to submit to the incomprehensible mystery of God, rather also as an element in the history of the experience of God in which God is seen in an ever more radical way as the mystery to be adored, to which we give ourselves in hope.

Both in my life and in my thinking I keep finding myself in situations of confusion which cannot be "cleared up". At first even I feel that one just has to carry on, even if one doesn't know where it's all leading. I feel that one must just keep quiet when one can't speak clearly, that carrying on in ordinary honesty is the only appropriate attitude for human beings, and the most that can be expected of us. But then I find I cannot avoid or keep silent about the question of what underlies this carrying on. What I find when I ask that question is the hope which accepts no limits as final. This hope concentrates all our experience into two words, "mystery" and "death". "Mystery" means confusion in hope, but "death" orders us not to disguise the confusion, but to endure it. I look at Jesus on the cross and know that I am spared nothing. I place myself (I hope) in his death and so hope that this shared death is the dawn of the blessed mystery. I must interpret death, and interpreting it as final emptiness and darkness has no more justification. But in this hope, even in all the darkness and disappointment, life already begins to emerge in its beauty and everything becomes promise. I find that being a Christian is the simplest task, the utterly simple and therefore heavy-light burden, as the Gospel calls it. When we carry it, it carries us. The longer one lives the heavier and the lighter it becomes. At the end we are left with mystery, but it is the mystery of Jesus. One can despair or become impatient, tired, sceptical and bitter because time goes by and the mystery still does not dawn as happiness, but it is better to wait in patience for the day that knows no ending.